■■■ Brownie Points

Brownie Points

Seven Steps to Success for Woman Entrepreneurs from One Who Made It

AUNDREA LACY

B2 BOOKS

AGATE

CHICAGO

Printed in Canada.

B2 Books is an imprint of Agate Publishing, Inc.

Library of Congress Cataloging-in-Publication Data

Lacy, Aundrea.
    Brownie points : seven steps to success for woman entrepreneurs from one who made it / by Aundrea Lacy.
        p. cm.
    Summary: "Drawing on the author's experience as a business owner, offers steps for overcoming obstacles to success faced by entrepreneurs starting their own companies"—Provided by publisher.
    ISBN-13: 978-1-932841-26-8 (pbk.)
    ISBN-10: 1-932841-26-1 (pbk.)
    1. New business enterprises—United States--Management. 2. Small business—United States—Management. 3. Entrepreneurship—United States. 4. Success in business—United States. 5. Businesswomen—United States—Biography. I. Title.
    HD62.5.L32 2007
    658.4'09082--dc22

2007008591

12 11 10 09 08 07   10 9 8 7 6 5 4 3 2 1

Agate books are available in bulk at discount prices. For more information, go to agatepublishing.com.

◆ DEDICATION

I want to dedicate my book to the closest person to my heart, "James," who has successfully fought AIDS for more than 10 years. Thank you for all of those late-night talks. I sincerely appreciate your steadfast love and support.

To my mentor, Mama Kake—you are so wonderful. I am so lucky to have someone like you in my life.

To my adorable son, Mateo—you are my sunshine. You are truly God's gift. I love you!

A NOTE ON LANGUAGE

I hope you will find this book friendly and easy to read. I have deliberately used a conversational style, including the occasional use of contractions where they fall naturally in the rhythm of a sentence.

To avoid stating "his or her" when giving examples, I have chosen to alternate between "his" and "her" pronouns from one example to the next.

The following are all registered trademarks of the Luv's Brownies company:

- Luv's Brownies® (brownies shaped like hearts)
- Luv Bites® (bite size heart shaped brownies)
- Home of the Original Heart-Shaped Brownie!®
- Give from the heart...give Luv's Brownies!®

TABLE OF CONTENTS

Foreword

Aundrea Lacy has a passion for life and the tenacity to succeed. From her example, which is spelled out in this book, you will be able to visualize and reach your professional goals, surmount personal obstacles, and build a strong business from the bottom up.

The success of her bakery shows that planning and persistence pay off. Despite great personal challenges, Aundrea has held her life and business together. I admire her spirit and work ethic, and I think you will too.

I frequently tell young people to face the world's challenges with a Triple Offense: something to touch head, hands, and heart. That's a perfect description of this highly motivating book. And her brownies are fabulous!

COACH KEN CARTER

▶ *Coach Ken Carter made national news in 1999 when he locked his undefeated Richmond High School varsity basketball team out of the school gym when team members failed to maintain acceptable grade point averages. His ultimate success with achieving the goals he had set for the team became the basis for the 2005 Samuel L. Jackson film* Coach Ken Carter. *For the latest news about his speaking engagements and the Coach Ken Carter Foundation, see www.coachcarter.com.*

Where the Luv Comes From

I found myself in need of some direction in my life. And that's when I went to my spiritual place and got still, and I listened for that little voice to speak to me. And thank God I did. That little voice said "Luv's Brownies—brownies shaped like hearts." I hope to inspire others as I have been inspired. Do not listen to negative voices. Only listen to the little voice that comes from within.

I wrote this book after receiving thousands of letters from customers who asked me how I had faced my challenges. I want you to know that you can start your own business if you put your mind to it. I hope that by sharing my story with you, I can spare you some hardships along the way.

I have always tried to learn from my mistakes and struggles. In fact, my award-winning brownie recipe was created by mistake—it was an accident caused by my dyslexia. I had to struggle to get James the medical treatment he needed when he was close to death. But I believe some trials and tribulations in life are truly blessings in disguise.

There is never a perfect time to do anything—starting a business, going back to school, or whatever. There will always be challenges and obstacles ahead. But don't let anything or anyone stop you from making your dreams a reality.

My Beginnings

Some trials and tribulations in life are actually blessings in disguise. I will never forget what it was like to feel slow or stupid in elementary school, high school, and college—never knowing the problem was a handicap called dyslexia. I always knew something was wrong, but I didn't know what it was.

I was born in a charming house next to Golden Gate Park in San Francisco. As our family grew, we resettled in San Bruno, a town of average working families on the peninsula, about six miles south of the big city. My two brothers and I were the only black children in San Bruno's schools for years. Our first house was down on San Bruno's "Avenues," near the train tracks, but as my father's business prospered, we kept changing houses until we were up in the hills, in an area of town called Crestmoor.

The Crestmoor house was a Japanese-style split-level that had been featured in *Better Homes and Gardens* magazine. At its heart was a state-of-the-art kitchen with a double oven and glass-topped range, which was next to an all-glass sunroom with a spectacular view of the entire San Francisco Bay Area. I remember watching airplanes arrive and depart as I ate breakfast and dinner.

My mom worked a swing shift as a housekeeper in a local hospital, so she couldn't do as much around the house as she would have liked to. (But you can bet that she taught me to keep a place clean—hospital clean!) That meant Daddy did most of the cooking.

Sunday mornings, before the five of us went to church, my dad would make us a hearty breakfast, including biscuits or pancakes from scratch; at the same time, he'd start dinner in a slow cooker. He was always planning ahead. My Mississippi-born father had a knack for cooking Southern-style meals around the clock—chicken and dumplings, banana bread, bread pudding, candied yams, collard greens, smoked turkey, sweet potato pie—you name it. There was always a wonderful aroma in the house.

As a kid, I had no idea how much careful planning my father had to do to make everything come out on time; I took it for granted, even as I picked up the habit. Later, I realized that it was from Daddy, and not my college business courses, that I learned the importance of "repeatable processes."

I hosted a dinner party one night during my first semester at San Jose State University. My guests expected me to order pizza or cook something simple like spaghetti—the usual student fare. Instead, I made a roast, candied yams, collard greens, and cornbread. Everyone thought my dad had made it! Planning pays off. From the time I first started my own business, running back and forth to my day job, I've always frozen some of whatever I prepared so that there is home-cooked food available at short notice whenever I need it.

It Runs in the Family

It's clear to me now that Daddy's example also taught me about being an entrepreneur—he owned his own business for 35 years. After returning from the Vietnam War in 1970, he attended the Academy of Art University in San Francisco and later opened his own hair salon. Two Saturdays a month, he would host a fashion show at the shop or at the Fairmont Hotel in the city; he designed and created all the gowns and even styled the models' hair.

Even now, I'm not sure how my father did it all—managing the salon, designing and creating dresses, preparing dinner every night, dropping us off and picking us up from school, and so forth. But I did see that it can be done, and that you can weave together all the responsibilities of work, home, and family.

Overcoming Challenges

So there I was, learning the lessons of kitchen and shop, my father's child—motivated, full of energy, and willing to work hard. Why wasn't I doing better in school?

During my graduating year at San Jose State University, when my counselor looked at my transcripts and realized I had failed the same algebra class five times, my grade point average was 1.98. He recommended that I be tested for a learning disability.

When the Disabled Student Services tested me, they learned I had the habit of transposing numbers—writing 65 instead of 56...and that sort of thing. That is why school—especially math—had been so difficult for me. I hadn't noticed the problem while cooking at home, because I learned from Daddy, who never measured anything numerically and just added ingredients by eye and experience.

We learn and improve when we can see that extra effort brings better results. But no matter how hard I tried at math, a little brain-cell sabotage along the way kept me from getting good results, so I could see no way to improve.

Even my cooking had suffered from the problem. Once I left home and started making new dishes, I discovered that you can't just wing it when it comes to measuring ingredients. I would buy any eggs that were on sale, but soon realized that the difference between medium and large eggs, for instance, makes a huge difference in a batter. So I started to pay attention to the numeric measures in recipes—and wound up transposing some of the numbers.

But half my problem lay in not knowing that there was a problem. When you know you have dyslexia, you can double-check and guard against it. And you can regain confidence in yourself.

After the Disabled Services assessment, the university decided to allow me to take a critical thinking course instead of fulfilling the math requirement. My counselor petitioned the university to lift some Fs from my record, and others were changed to credit/no credit.

Once the mystery of my disability had been solved, the hard work I'd always put in finally paid off. My graduating semester grade point average was 3.4, and the university presented me with an Outstanding Academic Achievement Award.

Charting a Path: Where the "Luv" Comes From

Now I just had to face the same mystery as everyone else—where to find the career I was meant to have. I longed to find one that would provide both a good living and personal fulfillment.

So I tried out many kinds of jobs in the marketplace: customer service, marketing communications, and project management for a Fortune 500 computer corporation; self-employment as a model;

and advertising and marketing for a Silicon Valley start-up. Sometimes I worked several jobs at a time, and sometimes I went to school on the side.

I was on my way out the door after work one night and ran into a colleague and friend. I had recently made him some brownies as a thank-you gift, and he stopped me at the door to tell me how good they were. I didn't tell him that under the stress of all the things I had to do, I had inadvertently transposed some of the numbers in the recipe. I'd doubled the amount of chocolate—and created a new recipe by accident. I'd felt terrible about the error, but my friend's pleasure with the brownies made me feel better.

When I got home that evening, my mind was racing with frustration. My work-school cycle was exhausting and seemed futile. I couldn't clearly see where I was going, or what my future held. I wondered whether or not all my hard work was achieving any purpose.

Ultimately, I decided to lie on my bed and pray. I prayed all night. During my reverie, I resolved to stop beating myself up over the error in that brownie recipe—the brownies had turned out great, they had come from the heart, and my friend had loved them. I happened to be looking at a favorite childhood doll at that moment, a doll named "Luv"—and suddenly, I heard a voice in my head say, *"Luv's Brownies—brownies shaped like hearts."*

Inspiration! I immediately decided to do research on what it would take to open a bakery. Instantly, all of my Silicon Valley customer service and marketing experience came to mind. I knew from the beginning that it would be an Internet bakery.

Once I completed extensive research on the enterprises of Mrs. Fields, Famous Amos, and countless others, I decided I wanted to own the business and not the bakery itself. My Internet business model would be based on renting space in a commercial kitchen. I spoke with my accountant, who advised me to contact Kathy MacDonald of Kathy's Kreative Kakes, a bakery owner who rented her kitchen by the hour. Mama Kake quickly became my mentor and one of my best friends; she has helped me through many challenging times.

At first I moonlighted with the bakery and maintained a day job in high technology, additional work modeling for print ads, and an existence as a full-time student working on an undergraduate degree. I missed out on a lot of social engagements, but I did not regret one day of owning my own business—even during endless nights when I was up for 24 hours baking, wrapping, and delivering.

I couldn't believe I turned my brownie recipe mistake into a business. I had been transposing numbers for years. I never imagined I would own an award-winning bakery. Being diagnosed with dyslexia was a blessing in disguise.

My Greatest Challenge

I continued to stay prayerful and ask for God's assistance, and soon I would need it more than ever. One day, I received a phone call that changed my life: A family member told me that someone very close to my heart was gay and had been diagnosed with AIDS.

"James," as I will call him, had been a loving supporter and the closest person to me throughout my life, but he had always hidden something inside. Now he had AIDS, and the roof had fallen in.

The hardest part for me in dealing with James's illness was seeing how AIDS victims are perceived—and avoided—by others. James was shunned and ostracized. (Even today, with his life and day-to-day health rebuilt, he has asked that I not use his real name.) This disease can't be contracted through a handshake or a conversation, but I was completely amazed at how people began to treat him—and me. So many people were afraid to shake his hand or hug him. I was never afraid to sit beside him, hold his hand, and feed, bathe, and clothe him.

At this point, I realized ignorance is everywhere, and I got angry about it. It was the right thing to get angry about, because the best way to fight ignorance is with knowledge—and knowledge is what eventually saved James.

When James entered the hospital, he was 6'0" and 190 pounds. Nine months later, he was 5'10" and weighed 150 pounds. His veins collapsed. His body became so dehydrated that he couldn't cry or sweat. He didn't have mucus in his nose, saliva in his mouth, or wax in his ears. He had a sore on his arm that took nine months to heal.

Not one doctor believed James was going to live. As the person closest to him, I was asked to find his birth certificate, pull all his life insurance papers together, and help prepare his last will and testament. And suddenly, I realized that after everything we had been to each other, I would never get the chance to tell him everything I wanted to say.

What I Could Do About It

I decided to get organized and do what I could to save him. Every day I monitored his progress, and I put together a spreadsheet of all of his medications so I could monitor them as well. At one point, he was taking 32 pills a day. Even so, I knew that I was not doing enough. I was just playing defense, following along with and keeping track of a course of treatment that simply wasn't working. I began to do independent research.

The word "research" scares some people. It reminds them of high-school term papers. But it's really one of the most basic survival skills you can develop—and it's not that difficult. If you approach it with the right attitude, it's a completely natural process. You go to the right place, and ask the first and simplest question you have. The answer will lead you to new questions and new places to ask them. As you progress through each step in the research process, you work with the answers you receive and break them down into simpler terms, until you're sure you understand them.

Any public library will be happy to help you. Every library has employees who are able to show you the research tools they have at their disposal, including Internet access. Believe me, they're usually happy to get involved in your problem—whatever it is—and help you find out all you can about it.

When I tackled the issue of James's treatment, I stayed focused. I knew I couldn't turn myself into a virologist or pathologist or any other kind of doctor just by reading articles in the library. But I could find out what was being done for AIDS victims who were getting better, and compare that with what was being done for James.

When I compared my findings to the medications listed in my spreadsheet and his treatment charts, I realized he wasn't on any medication to combat the disease itself—the medications were only treating its symptoms.

I questioned his doctors, and they soon conceded that I was correct. James was not on a "cocktail" medication to fight the AIDS virus.

My research experience as a student and as an employee of high-tech business had helped me discover the problem, and my practical experience at college and in the bureaucracies of business helped me cut through the red tape and get James the right treatment.

Today, I am happy to report that despite 11 years of full-blown AIDS, James looks and feels great. If anything, people take him for younger than his years—and believe me, he is always tickled to hear that. His illness was a bad scare, an ordeal, and a challenge, but I see challenges as stepping-stones to a richer life. I discovered that what I had learned in business helped me face James's medical problems, and what I learned dealing with his illness—constantly monitoring the situation and the processes in use, and always looking for changes that could be made to improve the outlook—has, in turn, helped me in business.

Not Just Financial Rewards

I often receive e-mails and letters from customers who are interested in owning a bakery. I can't tell them it's an easy life. But when I worked in an office, I often noticed that some of my coworkers lived for the weekend and nothing else. That wasn't how I wanted to live.

Ideally, you should enjoy your job so much that you don't care if it's Friday or if it's Monday—because you want to be there. And I can honestly say that's true for me. Over the past 11 years, I've never worried about failing or succeeding—because I love what I am doing.

I never wanted to hear myself say, "What would have happened if I had done X? What if I had tried Y?" Fundamentally, on a personal level, I needed to know that the girl who had felt so incapable in grade school could be successful at building a business from the ground up.

Passing the Lessons Along

So the challenges continue. I still consult in the high-tech arena. While doing consulting work, I learn exciting new integrated marketing communications techniques that I can use for the strategic plan and tactical elements of my own Internet business.

Many examples you will see in this book are drawn from my own experience in the baking business, of course, but I've also drawn heavily from the experiences of others. I've included instructive stories about some of the biggest corporations in America—companies that often wind up making the same mistakes small businesses are tempted to make, only on a much greater scale and with more obvious negative results. From time to time, I will use fictitious would-be entrepreneurs as examples of particular problems and solutions. These characters are based on people I've met as I've traveled the country and talked to groups of girls, women, and minorities on topics of self-employment and entrepreneurship. I've learned from them, and I think you will too.

Today, I'm concentrating on what I call the Three Bs of my business: my bakery, my book, and my baby doll Luv. It's all fun. And all of it is grounded on seven steps to success that I've identified.

One of the most rewarding things about learning these seven steps is the chance to pass them on to others. If you've read this far, you know where I've come from and how I came to start my business. I have written this book because I want to motivate you to do your own thing despite all the obstacles you may encounter.

You will always face challenges, but they should not stop you from making your dreams a reality. In the chapters to come, I will share with you what I've learned from keeping Luv's Brownies® alive and well through the Internet bust and beyond.

The Seven Steps to Success

Step 1. Starting from Zero. At this stage, you will learn when and how you should branch out into your own business, what preparations you can make if you're still in school, whether or not you should quit your day job, and related issues.

Step 2. Organize Your Life, Your Priorities, and Your Work. Your preparations and plans will come to nothing if you're drowning in details and can never figure out what to do next. But once you're organized, you can do more than you ever thought possible. I'll show you how to make this change in one day.

Step 3. Understand and Plan Your Finances—Both Personal and Business. Many beginners find financial planning daunting, but you'll see that you have little to fear.

Step 4. Start Small and Create a Solid Business Plan Around Something You Love. The most important thing that you can understand about your business is what it *isn't*. You must discard many false ideas that the world has about business enterprises before you can truly see your business clearly.

Step 5. Design and Document Repeatable Processes. Every business operation can be broken down into a series of small processes. This step shows you how those processes can be refined and recorded so every employee can look up the right way to do them, every time.

Step 6. Design an Integrated Marketing Campaign. This focuses on the conventional topics of sales, marketing, advertising, and promotion. I will keep the focus on the new small business, with special attention to the situation of entrepreneurs who are women.

Step 7. Get Still and Listen to that Little Voice. The preceding steps will prepare you to deal with all the challenges the external world will throw at your business every day. But when it comes to making decisions about the future, you have to stay connected with the internal and personal needs that your business is meant to serve. You have to make time to step into your spiritual space and listen for the little voice that comes from within. That little voice, the inspiration for beginning your business, will be with you before you even start Step 1. But don't leave it behind. Your final step is to stop and listen every day, and let that voice continue to guide you as you nurture and grow your business.

I sincerely hope that the principles and strategies in the pages that follow will help you find your own best path to success and make your dreams of self-employment and entrepreneurship a reality.

Starting from Zero

Believe me, I know about the dream of starting your own business and being an entrepreneur. I dreamed it myself and was determined to live it; now, I do live it, and most of the time, I love it. But I've lived the reality of it, too. I'm not about to step on your dream, because I want to help you achieve it—but there's no way to fully enjoy the business you've dreamed of until you've embraced the reality that goes along with it. So here goes.

The Dream

In no particular order, here are some of the advantages that you might think you will realize if you start your own business:

    1. You will be free of the rat race. No more following a rigid schedule, with no flex-time and few vacations. No more fear of layoffs. No more taking orders from bosses you don't like, or who don't like you. You'll be your own boss, so you obviously won't have to fear being fired. You'll set your own hours and schedule your own vacations. You won't have to accept any limitations that others might want to put on you because of your race, your gender, your religion, your appearance, the way you dress, or any disability you may have.

    2. You can work at home if you want to. You'll get to see your kids grow up and maybe you'll even home-school them. You can do everything over the phone and the Internet without changing out of your bathrobe. You won't have to waste time and money commuting to work.

3. The business will take off, and so will your earnings. When you're a wage slave, there's always a ceiling to what you can earn, but when you're self-employed, the sky's the limit. And once the big bucks start rolling in, there will be fame, too—your face on the cover of *Forbes* and your life story featured on talk shows.

4. After the fun comes the big buyout offer. And finally, no matter how much you've enjoyed being a CEO, one day some international corporation will offer you more millions than you can turn down, and you will sell the business and take a well-earned vacation on your yacht, or maybe a trip into outer space.

Okay, so that last part is a little over the top. But that's the dream, and we've all had some version of it.

The exact version you have can make a big difference, though. You need to think hard about this, and I'll tell you why.

What Are You Really Dreaming About?

Once, when I was 17 years old, I locked myself out of my car in a small town. I found a local locksmith in the yellow pages and left a message on his machine; after a while he showed up in his van. Getting my door open was like a game or a puzzle to him, and he cheerfully kept trying different methods until one of them worked. All the while, he told me his life story—how he had been a corporate lawyer who made lots of money but had to work 70 or more hours a week.

After his workaholic ways eventually led to a nasty and expensive divorce, he chucked it all. He moved to a small town and started a locksmithing business; he'd learned the basics from his uncle as a child for fun. And it was still fun for him. He didn't try to compete with the other locksmith in town when it came to making keys or installing locks in doors. He was hardly ever in his shop. He just took all the emergency lock-out calls because they usually came up at night, after he'd returned home from a day of fishing, and he enjoyed being the hero and figuring out the locks.

Without a doubt, he was one of the happiest men I've ever met.

But if you think he was living your dream of being self-employed, I have to say, "Wake up."

That isn't a dream of self-employment. It's a dream of *retirement*. My locksmith friend was not an entrepreneur. He was a retired man who'd saved money from his lucrative career. He was able to fill the days of his retirement with a fun hobby that paid him pocket change. If he hadn't had a lot of money banked from his days at the law firm, he wouldn't be making ends meet—not even close. Save that version of the dream for your golden years.

No dream comes true without hard work. Some weeks I work more than 80 hours.

The Reality

Rat race? Being the boss *and* the employee means you work twice as hard. You are in charge and responsible for everything. Your schedule may well wind up being even more demanding than your old day-job schedule because there will be so much to do. And you might not be able to fire yourself, but your customers can fire you by not showing up. I have to tell you this sooner or later: most small businesses fail.

Depending on what type of business you decide start, yes, you may be able to do it entirely from home. But don't ignore the drawbacks. You'll get to see your kids grow up, all right. But unless you're very careful, you will get to see them scribble crayon all over your invoices, and you will get to hear them demand you play with them and attend to their needs every single minute of the day. Carving out your own place and your own time for your work is not easy. And even if you have complete control of your children—or if you don't have any children—you will still have to control yourself. Being within arm's length of the refrigerator, the couch, the television, and the Internet all day can lead to wasting time and accomplishing nothing.

Will your business take off? There are strong odds that it will fail. With sound preparation and hard work, you can do your best to avoid it. But it's still likely that you will have to struggle for years before you can take a step back and call your business a success.

If your idea of success is being a hotshot CEO with thousands of employees working in big brick-and-mortar buildings that you own, the odds break against you again, because that's a lot of overhead to carry.

Magazine covers and television appearances are fun, if you like that sort of thing (and I do). But I can tell you from personal experience that you'll probably be too busy filling orders after the publicity to spend much time basking in the admiration of people on the street.

What about that idea of the friendly takeover—the opportunity to sell your name, image, and business to a big corporation for millions? It happens to very few. It's difficult enough to make a business last 11 years under your own management. And have you ever noticed that many people who do sell their names, their famous cookie recipes, their original pizza ideas, or their unique ice-cream flavors to other people for millions often wind up trying to go back into the same business all over again rather than retiring? Either they didn't make such great retirement deals after all, or they actually prefer to work. That's more proof that your dream should be about *enjoying your work.*

Don't Be Discouraged

Once you face these hard truths and embrace them, a lot of the dream is still there and within reach. Yes, you will work long hours, but you will have more control over them when you're your own boss, and that does feel good. You'll have to satisfy your customers and the bottom line, but that's almost always easier than having to satisfy the personal whims and prejudices of a boss. That's one reason why so many small businesses are launched.

Many new entrepreneurs are women. Why? Because despite all the odds, starting your own business is still the traditional way to make it in America—and it's one of the best ways to become successful. Even if you're not a woman, you can learn something from considering the workplace from a woman's point of view. Ask yourself, "Do I want to juggle a work schedule, home responsibilities, and so on, or do I want to take my chances and build something I can pass on to my children?" It's exciting and energizing to know that the sky *is* the only limit, even if you never reach it—it means that the promise and pleasure of the dream will always be there.

You Can Avoid the Biggest Pitfall

One of the reasons this step is called "Starting from Zero" is because you should plan to take baby steps from your starting point. One of the biggest self-employment mistakes that you can make— the heartbreaking story behind many small business failures—is gambling all your savings to buy into a "turnkey operation." The promise of "turnkey operations" is that you can buy a business the way you'd buy a car, with every component already in place and ready to go at the turn of a key. There are always people out there ready to sell you a franchise, a shop with an established clientele, a scheme to make money farming nutria or earthworms in your basement, or a position as an "affiliate" to a successful Internet-based business.

Some of these offers are outright scams, of course. Yes, the promoters will promise you that customers are already lined up for those earthworms, but all you have to do is look up their companies in an Internet search engine and see what its existing customers and franchisees have to say about them. The law takes a while to catch up to scammers, but their victims get on the Internet to spread the word right away.

Use your common sense. Many business scams are basically chain letters that offer you something for nothing—and nothing's exactly what you'll get. Yes, many successful businesses on the Internet have affiliate programs. Yes, if you put an ad for one of those businesses on your own website, and people click on it and buy the business's product, you might receive a small percentage from the sale. And yes, you can join 100 affiliate programs and put 100 ads on your website. But who is going to go to your website to look at 100 ads? You won't make money—unless people are already coming to your website because of something valuable that you offer there, something thousands and thousands of people want to see because you have been putting all your effort into creating it. You never get something for nothing.

Consider this offer: "You just buy the business and the orders will come in every day, effortlessly." Why would anyone sell such a lucrative and easy business to you? Why wouldn't they keep it for themselves?

Some turnkey offers are perfectly legitimate, but even they can spell disaster. It's true that every successful fast-food outlet was up for sale at one time or another; but not every franchise outlet succeeds, and those that do succeed because of hard work. And there are business owners interested in selling their stores or salons or inns so they can relax and retire, and some of these sellers are actually telling the truth about how much money their enterprises bring in and can prove it. But that's no guarantee at all that *you* can keep the business profitable.

If you have no previous experience with a particular kind of business, you *will* make all the usual beginner's mistakes. It's a fact of life, and you must accept it. Many people underestimate how many hours their business's previous owners put into it. And never forget that a good deal this year can turn sour the next year—what if road construction in front of your business makes your shop practically inaccessible for months, or if a crime wave in your store's area keeps shoppers away? Entrepreneurship is all about risk, of course, but you shouldn't have to risk your life savings. It's better to start from zero and take baby steps toward your goal.

Later on, when you've got experience running a business— whether it's your own or one in which you've worked your way up to a responsible position—it becomes more reasonable to think of buying an operation outright. Even in that case, however, it's best to stick to the kind of business you've already learned.

I'm not saying that you have to wait until you've worked your way up to the top of the ladder in your current job before you can think about starting your own business, or that the business you start has to be in the same line of work as the one you're currently in. Instead, I'm arguing for an entirely different course. The better way to go is to keep your day job at first while starting your own business—whatever kind you want, whatever your talents and interests suggest to you—on your own time, in a small way.

You're still betting on yourself, but it's a small bet—usually not much more than some hours of your time—and if it doesn't pay off, you can try another until you find one that wins. Meanwhile, your day-job paycheck keeps coming in.

You might say that two jobs will take up much more time and require much more scheduling? Yes, they will. But you might as well learn time management now—when you haven't bet your house on it—than later. When you shift to working at your own business full-time, it's probably going to be for just as many hours, and you won't have a separate boss looking after the schedule. But as soon as you find that product or service that people actually want, you'll be getting two incomes, too, and you can put some of that money aside for the day you become completely independent.

You Are Uniquely Qualified to Do This

Invariably, when I make these points when talking to new entrepreneurs, a listener will get the idea that I'm telling her to give up. "Starting your own business must take some kind of superwoman," she might say. "An average person like me doesn't have what it takes."

But there's no such thing as an average person. "Average" just applies to a group of people lumped together. As an individual, you have inherited certain qualities genetically and have acquired others through various adventures and lessons during your years on earth. What the world values most is what is most scarce, and there is no one quite like you on the face of the earth. You are not average. You are unique.

In my opinion, entrepreneurs who undervalue themselves are usually undervaluing their experience.

Consider this example of a young woman who might approach me after a talk. Let's say she's a 25-year-old a high school graduate with no college experience. We'll call her Dru.

Dru says, "I design my own jewelry, and people seem to like it.

Many of my friends have bought pieces from me, and they've told me that other people have asked them about the jewelry. I'd really like to make a business out of it. But all I've ever done is entry-level phone-based customer service for a mail-order house, temp work at travel agencies, customer service in the lingerie department of a store—that sort of thing. I've never taken any kind of business class, and I don't have any business experience at all."

"How can you say that?" I might reply. "There's no business in business school. Business is what happens on the front lines, where customers buy products and services, and that's exactly where you've been. A travel agency? So you've learned the importance of collecting precise information, you've seen how different price points and discount packages affect sales, and you've seen how businesses as different as hotels, airlines, and car rental agencies collaborate to make deals for potential customers. Customer service in a department store? That's one of the best introductions to customer relations that you can get, because buyers—and what makes them happy—are the same in every business. Your work on the telephone as a customer service representative is even more instructive, because you saw firsthand how the company you worked for succeeded or failed to respond to customer needs.

"In many family-run businesses, owners often bring their children into the business at 'the bottom'—working on the loading dock, as a messenger, or in an entry-level cold-call sales position. That's the best way to learn any business. My position taking telephone calls in customer service at Hewlett-Packard wasn't a high-status job—in fact, we were originally known as 'the call girls'—but soon I learned enough about the company's products to move into marketing and corporate communications. So many of the biggest producers in Hollywood started out working in the mailrooms of talent agencies that some Ivy League graduates fight for those 'entry-level' jobs! Dru, you've been witness to hundreds or thousands of customer transactions. If that isn't business experience, nothing is."

Perhaps there's an older woman standing next to Dru. Let's call her Irma.

Irma says, "That's okay for Dru. But I've been a stay-at-home mom for 22 years. Now that my kids are away at college, I want to pursue by own business, but I've never had what people call 'a real job' in my life. How do I get the skills I need?"

"Irma," I'd have to say, "Please. Everyone knows that 'mom' is one of the most demanding jobs there is. You've designed and maintained a budget and managed long-term financial planning for things like the kids' college expenses. You've kept up payments and paperwork for mortgages, loans, taxes, and insurance. You've kept a medical record on each child. You've been responsible for repairs and maintenance for every part of your house and your car. You've learned to motivate an immature and unwilling workforce to do chores and homework. I haven't even mentioned the usual cooking, cleaning, and chauffeuring that people associate with housekeeping, though of course every one of those tasks is a job as well. You've multitasked them all. You say you've never had a real job, but I say you have successfully managed a small business for 20 years."

Two of my primary messages are that *business lessons are life lessons* and *life lessons are business lessons*. To live and work is to solve problems, and learning to solve each problem makes the next one a little easier. Once you begin to apply your personal experience to your new business, you will quickly discover how much you already know.

Underestimating your experience is one of the two biggest psychological hurdles you have to get over on your way to self-employment. The other is fear of failure.

No one ever learned how to ride a bike or a skateboard without falling off. No one ever learns *anything* except by making a long series of mistakes and finding out how to correct and avoid them. George Washington lost most of the battles he ever fought in, but he won the Revolutionary War. Contemporary high achievers show the same pattern.

In 2006, television personality Barbara Walters devoted a show to the top 30 mistakes she had made in 30 years of broadcasting. It was nice to see someone of her stature acknowledge her growing pains. I've made one of the mistakes she mentioned myself: I once did an interview when I hadn't had enough sleep. One Valentine's Day, San Francisco radio personality Chuy Gomez interviewed me to announce the publication of my book *Luv Story*. I had been working furiously for the previous 36 hours—baking, wrapping, and delivering brownies. I was so tired that I couldn't even remember whether or not I'd eaten that day or the day before. Chuy asked me questions, and I must have answered them, but I have no idea what I said; he had to carry the whole interview. Fortunately, Chuy is a great guy and a skilled professional, and it wasn't the end of the world. But I learned to get a good night's rest before going on the air with an interviewer from then on.

The only way you can completely eliminate the possibility of failure is by never risking anything—and that means never doing anything. Instead, embrace the idea that you are going to make mistakes and that you will learn from them. My original brownie recipe was a mistake, but I looked for the blessing in that mistake and found it.

You simply have to start small—take small steps and small risks. Dru, the young woman who approached me after my talk, doesn't realize it, but she has already taken the first step toward building her own jewelry business. Selling or giving your products to friends and having them show them to other people is an excellent way to find out if there are enough potential customers to make the business work. You can start the same way.

Starting from School

Some of the most dynamic entrepreneurs I've ever met started their businesses while they were still in high school. There are more opportunities there than you might realize—many of them are of a nonprofit nature, but they allow students to gain experience with business and with the thrill of success.

School Fundraisers

A typical high-school business enterprise would be something like a bake sale, a car wash, or a dance to make money for a school club. That may sound small time to you, but the truth is that an enterprise like that has all the ingredients—and teaches all the lessons—of a small business. To organize and successfully pull off any of these kinds of events, you must carefully budget costs, find and motivate a workforce, realistically project how many customers you can attract, advertise and promote the event heavily, put the whole thing together on the day, and figure out how much to charge for the event (or the event's products) to make a profit.

With a school fund-raiser, you can usually enter at whatever level you choose. If you are willing to take on the responsibility, you'll either wind up running the show or being the right-hand person of whoever is running it. But if you've got less time to commit, event organizers will be happy to give you whatever responsibilities you can take on, and that will still give you a peek at the economics of the enterprise and a chance to learn practical lessons.

If you can run a few events like that in high school without actually losing money—and I'm not saying that's easy—you can step up to the next level in college or after high school, perhaps by organizing a concert with a well-known band. Doing so would mean making all sorts of connections with real-world businesses. You may have to book an arena instead of using a school gym, which also means making arrangements for insurance and security. You may produce newspaper and radio advertising, and you may find yourself working with the band's representation to generate interviews and other media events. An enterprise like this means more responsibility, more to keep track of, and a lot more stress in general—but you'll also learn a lot more, and you still aren't risking your own money.

A school fund-raiser can take many different forms. Some middle and high schools simply make arrangements with existing companies to sell products such as gift wrap, cookies, or magazine subscriptions, with students as the door-to-door sales force. The only thing a student can really learn from this sort of operation is "cold calling"—selling to people who weren't expecting you to ring their doorbells and who might not be crazy about the idea either. It's a chance to discover if you have a talent for this sort of face-to-face selling, which would certainly be useful in whatever future business enterprises you choose. But if you're not good at it, don't force yourself and don't worry about it. There are plenty of other ways to sell a product.

Business Mentoring Opportunities

There are other helpful organizations that cater to students. Junior Achievement (JA) is a nonprofit organization that brings a variety of different educational programs about entrepreneurship and markets into elementary and high schools. In addition to course materials for classes, JA also offers simulations, such as a board game called Risky Business. This game takes students through every stage of a start-up business over the course of five days: building the business plan, the necessary capital, and the team; developing products and finding money to manufacture them; analyzing the customer base and potential profit margin; and managing the initial public offering (IPO) of stock. Another JA program, Job Shadow, encourages local businesspeople to take students on personal tours of their workplaces, explain the nuts and bolts of their businesses, and possibly engage students in short- and long-term internships.

JA often works closely with the Teen Business Link program sponsored by the U.S. government's Small Business Administration (www.sba.gov/teens), which is also a solid resource for advice from actual businesspeople on how you or your club can start a small business while still in high school.

Recent success stories among JA entrepreneurs may give you ideas for your own business: landscaping; repairing computers; teaching swimming, music, or dance; tutoring; and even more sophisticated work such as Web design.

If you do not have a JA branch at your school, call a local office for more information. Find out more at JA's website: www.ja.org.

Other national organizations also provide business mentoring, and often local retired businesspeople are interested in less formal mentor-student relationships. Your local chamber of commerce is the first place to check for volunteer efforts of this kind.

If at all possible, try to get involved with a program that lets students originate their own products or services instead of selling an existing line of products. One disadvantage of the business-school mindset is a tendency to stress marketing and advertising over actual product value, but invention, innovation, and superior workmanship are the real building blocks of a successful company. Even the best marketing and advertising can't keep an inferior product afloat for long.

Don't discount the possibility of manufacturing your own product, however primitive it might be. Remember that at your school, you may have access to the resources of a wood, metal, or print shop. Only by building your own products will you experience the full design, production, quality-control cycle that's at the heart of a real business.

Some mentors have so much fun reliving their glory days that they are tempted to take over your project. Don't let this happen. You won't learn anything as a passive observer; step up and take as much responsibility as you can.

Traditional Student Jobs Are Educational

Some of the entrepreneurial ideas commonly suggested to students, such as dog walking, lawn mowing, car washing, or babysitting services, may sound small time to you. But don't overlook their potential. The hourly pay is often as good as working in a store—sometimes better—and you gain the experience of running the show yourself.

Suppose you do work in a store or restaurant. That's one of the most common part-time jobs for high school students, and while it isn't entrepreneurial in nature, it's still a chance to learn valuable business skills. Remember what I told Dru. The front counter is also the front line of any business; if you keep your eyes and ears open, you can learn how the whole business works. And it's never too early to develop the right attitude toward customer service.

I frequently see young people working counters and cash registers like zombies. They're inattentive when they aren't downright rude, and their posture and body language communicates to customers, "I'm a nobody here, trapped in a boring job, and facing customers I can't stand." I'm not going to pretend that most retail jobs are fun and exciting—they aren't. But when you punish your employers and customers for your boredom, you're the one who suffers most.

Straightening up, smiling, and treating each customer's transaction as if it matters to you is professional behavior and part of giving an honest day's work for a day's pay. You'll find that it *feels* so much better than acting the part of a miserable prisoner. You'll be amazed at how much nicer and more pleasant the customers are when you give them courteous and friendly service.

Good bosses also notice. If you don't have a good boss and instead have a tyrannical fool with a shoddy and depressing operation, your professional attitude—which will stand out even more—can help you get another, better position. If I'm hiring store help and notice you're doing a great job behind the counter, I will hand you my business card and tell you to call me. A good businessperson always keeps an eye out for a good employee—and someday, you'll do it, too.

Another Bad Habit

At the risk of sounding middle-aged and uncool, I must now deliver a little lecture on cell phones and text messaging.

Don't get me wrong. I love my cell phone, and like most people, I can't imagine how I ever lived without it. But most new inventions have a downside, and the cell phone is no exception. The cell phone—or at least the situation of everyone owning a cell phone—is still fairly new, and as such there are few hard and fast rules about using them in a socially acceptable way.

I'm not going to rant about people who rudely shout into their phones in restaurants or cause accidents while they talk and drive. My concern is helping you on your best path to success and showing you how to develop the correct habits and strategies.

When I talk at schools and colleges, I often see students who begin and end each class with a frantic round of phone calls and text messages. From hour to hour, they are always touching base with a network of friends and family. "What happens next?" "Where do we meet?" "What will we do?"

I know this micromanaging of your social network *feels* important. Plans are being ironed out, appointments are made and broken, and time frames are established. But the truth is, when you have to check with a group of people every 20 minutes to find out what you're doing an hour from now, *you have no plan beyond that.* You're just being nudged along by the herd, like a sheep. You're not using the cell phone to manage your life; the cell phone is managing you.

Talking to your friends is fun. I could cheerfully schmooze for eight hours a day—you probably could, too—and now technology makes it possible to do just that. The problem is that while you're talking to your friends, you can't do much of anything else.

Phone addiction is not restricted to the young. I have known many executives in Fortune 500 companies who spend hours every day making redundant telephone calls to various team members, interrupting the work of others to ask them the same questions they've asked the previous day or leaving messages so their own work will be interrupted later by equally pointless callbacks. They think they're being productive, but the opposite is true.

There are times when a short call will eliminate the need for a long e-mail or letter, and of course sales calls are a necessity of business, but the average "I'm just going to touch base with Jill about that" call wastes your time and Jill's.

Nip this bad habit in the bud. Unless you work in a customer-service capacity, let an answering machine take your calls most of the time so you can work or study without interruption. Check your messages frequently and make necessary outbound calls during blocks of dedicated time, perhaps while taking care of other tasks that you can do without thinking (such as laundry or walking the dog).

You'll discover that you don't really miss much if you don't pick up every call. Initially, some of your friends or associates may express irritation that they can't always reach you in real time. Just remember that you're actually saving their time as well as your own. And because people value what is rare and desire what is hard to get, people will soon feel more respect for you and will try to get your attention with calls that are actually important.

Taking the Right Classes

A few classes may also be useful to a budding entrepreneur.

Typing. No matter what you do in the future, you will need to use a computer either personally, professionally, or both. Even if your household doesn't yet have a PC, you have undoubtedly had some hands-on training and computer access at school. But if you haven't yet taken a touch-typing or keyboarding course, do so now.

In my student days, I worked in my dad's hair salon sweeping up hair, washing towels, answering the phone, and making coffee. Occasionally, some of the customers would tell me to avoid typing courses because women who typed too well would get stuck in a typing pool and would never advance above that position. Even just 10 years ago, there were managers who never personally touched a keyboard. But this is a new century. When you're the CEO of your own small business, the PC itself is your secretary, and the faster and better you can use it, the more power it will give you.

If you're already out of school and are still typing by the hunt-and-peck method on your PC, buy a software course in keyboarding. These programs are inexpensive—one of the best, "Mavis Beacon Teaches Typing," is often bundled free with new computers—and they really work; you can double your typing speed after only a few weeks of practicing a half-hour a day. That's because the computer has the ability to sense which letters and fingers give you the most trouble as you learn, and it can give you extra help precisely where you need it. Some of the drills can be structured as video games, which makes the learning more fun.

You can also take courses like these at your public library. More and more public libraries allow you to use computers and the Internet. Sometimes all you need is a library card, and sometimes there's a small fee involved. I own a computer, but when it was recently infected with a virus, my local library saved my life.

Business and accounting. The most useful business-specific class you're likely to get a crack at in high school or the first year of college is Basic Accounting. Go for it. Most of us don't have the skills and mindset to become certified public accountants, but if you can just pick up the fundamental concepts, it will make a huge difference in your future business planning. At the very least, you'll know what your accountant is talking about.

What College Means

College is ridiculously expensive these days, and it's not because the quality of a college education has increased. It's because employers can no longer count on a high-school diploma meaning anything—not even the ability to read and write. Now only a college degree seems to guarantee those basic skills, so colleges can and do charge high prices because they know they'll have students, no matter what.

Don't believe you just need that "piece of paper," the diploma. If you have no idea what specific college courses will benefit you or what you want to do with your life, maybe the best idea for you is to postpone college for a few years and work in the real world. Many people wish they'd done so instead of wasting money and time taking college classes that turned out to be completely irrelevant to their subsequent careers. Just one year in the workplace might focus your interests and reveal to you what you really want to do for a living. The discipline you will learn in a nine-to-five job will help you succeed in college, which is a much less structured environment full of temptations to goof off.

Being an entrepreneur means thinking for yourself, educating yourself, and going your own way. Write your own college schedule.

Organize Your Life, Your Priorities, and Your Work

If you follow Step 1 and start from zero, taking low-risk baby steps along the way, your first self-employment experience as an entrepreneur is likely to be something you do on the side as a full-time student or as a working professional with another day job. You might be baking brownies, as I was, or minding babies, tutoring students, mowing lawns, typing papers, drawing caricatures, or designing websites—whatever is convenient, fun, and right for you.

What you're doing may resemble a hobby more than a business, and the good news is that until it starts making appreciably more money than it costs you, it *is* just a hobby as far as the IRS is concerned. Few other bureaucracies are likely to notice that you're operating a business either. But this will change.

Real Business, Real Complications

If you are reading this book, your intent is to create a real business and not just a hobby. Thus, your only choice is to embrace the complications that inevitably set in once you start making money, paying taxes, and observing regulations.

If you're offering a neighborhood service, for instance, like baby-sitting or lawn mowing, the most obvious route to expansion is to bring in additional workers. Yes, you'll have to share the proceeds with them, but it's still to your advantage, because you'll be able to expand your hours of operation and the number of jobs you can take on. Soon, customers will notice that while "Jack, the kid who mows lawns" is often booked up weeks ahead of time, "Jill's Landscaping" is always available. Six months later, you'll probably find that you're not cutting many lawns yourself; instead, you're handling the advertising, bringing in the customers, scheduling and guaranteeing the work, and hiring and if necessary firing personnel—you're the boss, and it's a business. You'll have to either start withholding payroll taxes from your workers or sign them up as independent contractors. Either way, you'll have to keep very careful records for your own taxes.

Taxes aren't the only concern, either. You'll probably need a state business license, and maybe another one for your city—especially if you work out of your home. Since these requirements vary, I can't advise you on them. Consult your local chamber of commerce, which should be able to answer your questions or point you to the state agency that can.

You will also discover that a surprising number of businesses and occupations require special licenses. In many large cities, for example, you can't drive a cab without purchasing a required "medallion" from the city for a large sum of money—tens of thousands of dollars, in some cases, and in New York City, hundreds of thousands of dollars. In most areas, performing beauty-related services, including doing nails and hair, generally requires completion of a training program and a licensing examination. If you're just braiding your friends' hair in your apartment, you can get away with it for a while, but you can't open a salon without a license.

In addition to taxes and licenses, your business schedule itself becomes far more complicated when you consider the number of workers and the number of customers. Workers may call in sick or quit with little notice; you will have to find someone else to do their work or find a way to satisfy the customer. If you want to take some time off yourself, you'd better put some backups on standby in advance and designate someone to take the sick calls in your absence.

As your business expands, you will face an increasing number of appointments, deadlines, and business letters that have to be answered. And what about your personal life? If you want one, you will have to schedule it.

So there's no way around it. You have to get organized.

The World of Organizing and Time Management

Hundreds of books have been written on this subject. You have a wide range of systems you can apply, and a choice of physical tools you can use to implement them.

The systems range in complexity and focus. David Allen's book *Getting Things Done: The Art of Stress-free Productivity* (Penguin, 2002) will help you reorganize your entire life; it even includes flowcharts to take the geek in you through the tasks and sub-tasks of his grand design. Julie Morgenstern's popular *Organizing from the Inside Out* series (Owl Books) takes a psychological approach and shows you how to build a system based on your personal style and goals. You can also choose Alan Lakein's classic *How to Get Control of Your Time and Your Life* (Signet, 1989), a simple but powerful system based on to-do lists. It's been around forever, so some of the language and examples are a little dated, but by the same token, you can almost always find a used copy for a dollar or less.

Most of these systems can be implemented with either a simple spiral notebook or a personal digital assistant (PDA), such as a Palm Pilot. You may also choose to let the layout of a particular brand of appointment book (such as Day Runner or Day-Timer) or personal information management software (such as Microsoft Outlook or Ecco Notes) tell you how to keep track of your contacts, appointments, and to-do information.

Every one of these systems and tools does a great job for some people; any one of them might be right for you. I have just two bits of advice:

- Do something to organize your time and paperwork as soon as you can.
- Don't try to do too much.

I've seen dozens of managers, workers, and homemakers who *think* they're organized because they maintain enormous lists of their tasks and projects and have completely filled a big calendar that tells them what extremely productive thing they will be doing from 1:45 to 2:15 p.m. three months from now. In fact, of course, none of them get *anything* done on time, because they waste so much of the day trying to prioritize those huge lists and because as soon as anything unexpected comes up, that whole three-months-into-the-future schedule is wrecked and has to be redone.

And some people never even get that far. They are always reading new books on organizing, buying new preprinted calendar inserts, and *planning to start planning* one of these days, but first—they tell you—they'll have to decide what system to use. And there are so many decisions to make. Before they can put all their papers into files, for instance, they have to label the files. How will they know what to put on the labels so that all the papers will have a logical place? The excuses go on and on.

If you think the world of organizing and time management looks like too much to deal with, I understand—but that simply isn't true. To prove it, I'm going to give you a stripped-down system that can organize your whole life and your business in this single chapter.

You can buy all the physical components for well under $100—$50, if you take the cheaper route. You can set the entire thing up in one weekend day. And from then on, your decisions—and your life—will be much easier.

The Must-Do System

Here are the advantages of the Must-Do system:

- Everything you *must* do *can* get done—on time. You know what you're supposed to do every day, and the list isn't ever more than you can do in a day. You'll have no stress from being too rushed and no more guilt from missed deadlines.

- Every piece of paper that enters your office gets properly processed—on time.
- Every piece of paper you will ever have to find again gets filed—quickly and easily—in exactly the place where you will look for it in the future.
- Every unessential piece of paper will be disposed of and will not slow you down as you search for the important stuff.

The system is simple and flexible. It doesn't try to plan your life from hour to hour for months into the future, so when an emergency strikes—or you just want to go to a movie—you have less to update and rewrite.

The system is based on standard strategies. If you get hooked on organizing once you see what it can do for you and decide to incorporate additional features from another time-management system, you won't have to change everything. You can simply add on to it.

So you've got nothing to lose, and everything to gain. Let's get started.

Must-Do: The Key Idea

What makes this system simpler than the others? The key idea of the Must-Do system. Most people get bogged down in organizing their time and projects when they set priorities—or fail to set them. It's easy to feel productive if you are busy every minute, rushing from one task to another depending on whatever pops into your mind at the moment. But you can quickly fill a day like that without actually tackling any of the important tasks that pay your bills.

The Must-Do system gets your priorities straight at the beginning of each and every day. It is entirely focused on getting top-priority tasks done first, because if you're juggling your own business, a day job, and a life with family and friends, there will be days when the top-priority tasks are all you have time for. When your schedule is less full and your Must-Dos are done, you can spend your time as you like with no guilt or stress, knowing that nothing serious is hanging over your head.

To get your priorities straight every morning, you have to master one simple concept—what is a Must-Do? A Must-Do, or top-priority task, is simply a task that must be completed by a particular deadline, or there will be serious negative consequences. If you do not pay your bills, your electricity, heat, and telephone services will be cut off, your landlord will start banging at your door, and you will ruin your credit. If you do not show up for a medical appointment, you will be charged for it anyway, and you'll still have to go at a later date. That last example means that a routine once-a-year checkup—something you might schedule for any month of the year—becomes a Must-Do once you make the appointment. Similarly, even fun stuff like meeting your friends for dinner and a movie becomes a Must-Do once you've made a definite date, because your friends will be upset if you fail to show up.

But notice that there is still flexibility within the Must-Do system. For example, you must do *something* about that dinner date, but you don't have to go. You can cancel, in which case the Must-Do is to cancel in a timely fashion, so your friends can also change their plans or at least know not to wait for you. Although your grocery shopping may not be a Must-Do today (when you still have a week's worth of food in the house), it will become a Must-Do when failing to do it involves negative consequences (no food in the house).

So a Must-Do is a deadline and appointment with a fixed end date and serious negative consequences if it is not acted upon. And that's all. There are many other things you would *like* to do, and some that you *will* do, but they are not Must-Dos that will be scheduled.

A sale at a store is not a Must-Do if you're just going there to see what you can find. There is no serious consequence if you don't go; in fact, if you don't go you'll save time and money. The sale might be a Must-Do if you have been waiting for a particular item at that store—an item you genuinely need—to be reduced in price by 50 percent; the serious consequence would be losing money (because you'd have to pay full price for the item later) or losing the chance to buy it at all. But be honest with yourself. If you don't really need the particular item, failure to buy it is not a serious negative consequence.

Things you do routinely every day—brushing your teeth, taking a shower, showing up at your day job—don't count as Must-Dos, but you will suffer serious consequences if you stop doing them. Most of them don't have a special deadline, and you're doing them already—there's no need to schedule them, and it would be a waste of time to do so.

With those routine tasks eliminated, if you're still coming up with 20 or 30 Must-Dos a day, then you aren't being realistic about the "Must" part. You aren't going to get that many things done anyway—you'd be lucky to finish half of them—and the consequences of real Must-Dos will hurt you when they fail to get done because you wasted time on the fakes.

When you're tough and realistic about what constitutes a genuine Must-Do, you'll find that there are really no more than 5 to 15 to do in a day, and sometimes fewer. This will free you up to take care of other things you would like to do, without guilt. Be rigorous, and always ask yourself these questions:

- Does this task have a genuine deadline, or would it just be nice to do it sometime soon?
- What will happen if I don't do it by the genuine deadline? Are there negative consequences?
- Are those consequences really that bad? Compared with, say, completely running out of money or food?

When you find yourself agonizing over priorities, it's because you're really not thinking about Must-Dos at all. What is hard is prioritizing the other stuff—what you wish you could do someday, what you'd really like to do before the summer ends, what sounds like fun and might be really great to do but you won't know unless you try, and so on. There's no magic formula that will tell you which of those things to do first. But with practice, genuine Must-Dos are easy to recognize—in your heart, you know what tasks are critical because of the consequences if you fail to do them.

Big Projects

So far, the discussion has focused on tasks, or things you can do in minutes or hours within the course of one day. Sometimes, however, there are projects that will require many days of work, or perhaps a few hours of work every day.

Consider this situation: Your boss asks you to complete a 25-page report by the end of the month. This project is a Must-Do, and there are negative consequences if you don't deliver, but making a note that it's due on September 30 isn't going to get it done if you forget about it until September 29.

To apply the Must-Do system to this type of assignment, set aside 10 to 20 minutes to consider the project in detail. Then break the project into separate tasks that can be done in a single day. For the project, a sample list of tasks could include:

- Research the topic on the Internet.
- Research the topic in the library.
- Write an outline.
- Write the first five pages.
- Write the second five pages.

Treat each of these tasks as a Must-Do and assign it a deadline, and treat that self-imposed deadline as seriously as any external Must-Do deadline. Yes, it doesn't seem at first that there's a serious negative consequence if you don't start research that first day; no one knows but you, and you think that you can make it up later. But each deadline you miss makes it harder to make the next one, and before you know it, you will fail to meet the project's final deadline. If you find it too hard to complete your tasks on time, divide the project into smaller chunks. But treat them all as Must-Dos.

Once you grasp the Must-Do concept, it's not hard to implement the whole system. You only need a few physical components:

- A calendar
- Three Must-Do lists
- One Wanna-Do list
- Three desk trays
- A file cabinet

The calendar. A big wall or desk calendar is probably good enough, as long is there is room to write several notes within a given day. A day planner or appointment notebook will fit the bill, too, but don't fixate on filling every slot on the calendar with appointments and tasks. This calendar is only for fixed appointments and permanent deadlines in the future—not for the details of your daily schedule.

Three Must-Do lists. These are what people usually call To-Do lists, except that they only include Must-Dos. The three lists are headed "Today," "Tomorrow," and "This Week." The "Today" and "Tomorrow" lists should not be very long, because there are only so many tasks you can accomplish in one day. (I won't say exactly how long, because depending on your business and your lifestyle, you might have many Must-Dos that can be accomplished quickly, or you might have fewer Must-Dos that take larger chunks of time.) The "This Week" list will be longer—especially at the beginning of the week—but it will get shorter and shorter as its items get promoted to the other two lists.

You can keep your Must-Do lists in any physical form that's convenient for you. You may choose to use a small spiral notebook, a few index cards, a computer, or a PDA. The important thing is to be able to consult and update them easily at any moment during the day.

The nice thing about keeping your lists on a PDA, your laptop, or a desktop computer is that the personal information management software lets you reorder items or move them from list to list without rewriting them; you just drag and drop. And if you use different computers at home and at work, but always have access to the Internet, you can keep your lists or calendar posted online. There are a number of websites where you can do this for free. Online to-do lists or calendars can be kept private with a password only you know—but if you work with a team, it can also be useful to keep a public version to which they have access; you can set up your web service either way, or both. Of course, you should occasionally print out a physical backup copy; you can make that a Must-Do item once or twice a week.

The Wanna-Do list. Using any of the same physical formats, you should also keep a longer list of things you would like to do if you find the time. The good news is that you *will* do some of these things—your life is not limited to a prison of Must-Dos. The bad news is that if you are living an average person's busy life, you will never accomplish *most* of these tasks. Face it, the world is full of many thousands, if not millions, of wonderful things to do, buy, use, and experience. It's easy to put them on a list, impossible to get around to them all. Even if you try to be realistic about your limits, your Wanna-Do list is going to keep growing steadily unless you regularly cut it back.

You will cut it back in two ways. You will make a commitment to a minority of Wanna-Dos and promote them to Must-Dos. You will judge a majority of Wanna-Dos less important than the others, cross them out, and let them go.

Three desk trays. They should be labeled "Today," "Tomorrow," and "This Week," and can be stacked on top of one another to save space. Any paperwork that comes into your office or home office that must be acted on that very day goes into the "Today" tray (if you can't simply act on it immediately). Any paperwork with a hard deadline for tomorrow, and that isn't convenient to do today, goes into the "Tomorrow" basket. Anything with a hard deadline for later in the week, or for the end of the week, goes into the third tray. Anything with a hard deadline further out gets its deadline written on the calendar, and is filed.

Your desk should always be clean. If an important paper isn't in one of those three trays, it should be in a file where you can easily find it when your calendar tells you to do so. The only paperwork that should be in front of you is what you are working on at that particular moment.

A file cabinet. We have now reached the only component of the Must-Do system that costs any money or time to set up. You are going to need files. The best kind are called "hanging files," and the best place for them is a steel filing cabinet. Such a cabinet can cost a hundred dollars or more, but you can get them cheaper for sale or used; every day, businesses that use file cabinets are liquidated.

You can also select a cheaper solution: stackable plastic file boxes that come with grooves for the hooks of hanging files; you can find these at retailers like Staples. However, you're better off buying a regular filing cabinet as a commitment to the system. Eventually, you will probably have more than one cabinet.

No matter whether you use a dedicated cabinet or stacked boxes, files will take up some space in your office. However, unfiled papers lying in clumps on every surface will cause you much more inconvenience, because you will have to search through every stack to find the paper you want. Unfiled papers take up more room physically than a file cabinet does, because, as you will see, the most important part of the filing process is throwing unnecessary materials away.

The file folders themselves cost money, too, but not much if you buy them in bulk—and you should. As you will see, the more files you have, the less time you will waste looking for things. Hanging files are the best because they are easy to move in and out of the drawer if you want to go a folder, and they don't spill open if there aren't enough files in the drawer to prop them up. But the most important thing about files is for each to have a clearly labeled tab that tells you what is inside. It's good to have tabs that aren't all lined up at the same place on the top of each file; if they are staggered across the tops of the files, you can read all the tab labels at a glance instead of having to thumb through them one by one.

Don't buy files with preprinted subject or alphabet labels on their tabs (unless you can get them especially cheap that way, in which case you can cover the printing with your own sticky labels).

It's important that you make up the subject labels yourself—but it isn't going to be hard, as I'll explain next.

Converting to the Must-Do System in One Day

I've mentioned that the Must-Do system takes only one day to set up. Most of that day will be spent filing all the bills, letters, magazines, and unclassifiable paper trash that is stacked all over your house or office. Don't panic! It won't be nearly as hard as you fear it will be, and you will only have to do it once.

Here's the process:

Bring all your loose papers and envelopes of associated papers into one room.

Do a preliminary sort into three big piles; if you have three large tubs or laundry baskets, use them to keep the piles from mingling. Anything that won't go into one of the three piles will go into the trash, so have a big trash bag ready, too. This first sort is as simple as it could be and will require little or no thought. If you find yourself bogging down and reading papers, stop, and get back to sorting.

The first pile is for "action items." These are papers you are keeping because you have to reply to them or take some other action on them. Action items include Must-Dos with deadlines and consequences—like bills or renewals—but also anything else that you currently intend to act on, even if there isn't a hard deadline or bad consequences for inaction. If you currently *intend* to do something about it, it goes in the Action pile. You can reconsider acting on it later; right now the idea is to get through the first sort as quickly as possible.

The second pile is for items you want keep for future reference, even though you don't have to take action on them. Some of these are Must-Keeps, like your birth or naturalization certificate, your business licenses, all your different insurance papers, the family recipes you use again and again, and so forth. Some are Smart-Keeps, like registrations, warranties, and instructions for household appliances or software applications. And some are just Wanna-Keeps, like treasured love letters or family memorabilia you can't bear to throw away. Fortunately, you don't need to spend one minute thinking about whether a given paper is a Must-Keep, a Smart-Keep, or just a Wanna-Keep. They all just go into the same pile for now; the important thing is to keep moving.

The third pile is for "Recreational Reading"—all those magazines, newsletters, or clippings you meant to read some day. These items aren't ones that you need to do anything about (if they were, they'd go in the Action pile) or that may be necessary for reference one day (those would go in the Keep file)—they are simply items that you'd enjoy reading once and don't want to throw away just yet. If you find that this pile is getting very large, I can tell you right now that you're never going to read most of those things—but that's okay. Don't think about it during the preliminary sort. Just put them in the Recreational Reading pile and move on.

If you've got no good reason to put an item in one of the three piles—if it is not something you need to act on, keep for future reference, or read once for pleasure—throw it in the trash. Period. There's no reason not to.

Don't forget to keep an eye open for duplicates. If you haven't paid your telephone bill for three months, you don't have to keep all three bills in your Action file; throw out everything except the last one, the one you will pay. If you always buy shoes from the same mail-order house, you only need to keep the latest catalog for reference; all the older ones are trash. You don't need to keep a warranty or manual for every toaster you've ever owned.

If you're not throwing out half the items you look at, then you are probably not being tough enough, and your Keep and Recreational Reading baskets are overloaded with things that should be trashed. But don't worry. That problem will be corrected in the next stage of sorting. Just keep going until there are no items left and every last thing is sorted or thrown away.

Recreational Reading

Let's start with the least important stuff first: Recreational Reading. If this has never been a big category for you, you may only have a small pile of a dozen or so magazines, newsletters or clippings. Great! Find a place on a bookshelf or under a coffee table to put that pile and you're done with this category. However, if you're habitually a recreational reader, you may have a basket full of items. But if that doesn't bother you, and you have a place to put the basket, great. You're done in that case, too. Either way, there's a rule you have to follow in the future.

Every time you bring a new magazine into your space because you think you want to read something in it once, you must either read it that day or take it to the Recreational Reading pile. And if you go to the pile, you must remove from the pile something you want to read less than the new item and throw it away. If there's nothing in the pile you want to read less than the new magazine you're holding, throw the new one away. You already have plenty of good stuff to read when you feel like reading, and you haven't been getting around to it. From now on, you don't add to that pile. And if it really is a basketful, you might think of throwing out two items for every one you add, until it's down to a reasonable size.

Now let's suppose that after the rough sort, you don't have just one basket of Recreational Reading, but a huge pile—two or three baskets worth. That's too much. There's no reason to stock up that far ahead. Harden your heart and cut it down. A fast way to do so is to throw out every item that's over a year old—you'll be surprised how many are.

Remember not to bog down the sorting process by reading the material you're sorting. You can make your decisions on the basis of a magazine's table of contents, or by an article's title and first paragraph—that's usually all that interested you in the first place. Try not to spend more than an hour on this final sort, no matter how big the pile is. Remember, if the pile is too big, there is little chance you'll ever actually read what's in it. If the pile is small, on the other hand, you're far more likely to actually read and enjoy the articles; and if that isn't what it's about, why keep them at all?

Filing the Keepers

This is the part you have been afraid of, but there is really no need to be—filing your keepers is a simple, logical process.

If people think filing is hard, they probably think they have to write out all the different categories for labels in advance. Usually they have bought too few files and labels and think, "How can I cover every possible type of paperwork with only 12 or 20 categories?" Or "Well, I'll have 26 files labeled A-Z and will file everything alphabetically. But that will mean a million decisions, like: 'Does Bill's business license go under 'Bill,' or 'Licenses,' or 'Business Licenses,' or the name of Bill's business?'"

This sort of top-down procedure of guessing the best categories and making the papers fit never works. It takes forever, and when you're done, you still won't have any confidence that you can find anything.

Instead, you will file from the bottom up, making file categories fit the papers you actually have. This means you'll have a larger number of files, but that's the only price you'll pay for a system that will let you find everything fast.

Creating files. Randomly pick a paper or envelope full of related papers out of the keeper stack. Let's pretend it's the recipe for the Thanksgiving stuffing you make every year. Pick up a file, put a label on it, and fill out the label: "Recipes." Put the recipe in the file and hang the file in the top drawer of the cabinet.

Pick up the next keeper. Perhaps it's your car insurance policy. Take a new file and label it—what? Anything that strikes you as logical and specific enough is good enough. "Insurance" would work, if you think all your different insurance papers will fit in one folder. If you have a great deal of insurance and think you will need more than one file to hold all the paperwork, then "Car Insurance" would probably be a better choice. Perhaps it would make more sense to you to file all of your car-related materials together, so you'd label the file "Car" and use it for your car's registration, purchase and maintenance records, and insurance paperwork. If that seems simple and logical to you, do it, and don't spend much time thinking about other ways you could label it—there is no one right way that you have to discover.

All your file label has to do is answer one simple question: *If I were looking for this piece of paper, would I know that it was in this file and no other file?* Keep asking and answering that question as you go along, and you can't go wrong.

File names don't have to be formal or businesslike: they just need to make sense to you. For example, perhaps you'll come across a brochure about inexpensive places to stay near Disneyworld. You're keeping it because you're planning a Disneyworld trip, and somewhere in your big pile of keepers there are 10 to 20 other brochures or clipped articles with helpful information on the subject. So call this file "Disneyworld Trip" or "Disneyworld Stuff" or even just "Disneyworld". If you were looking for this information, wouldn't you find it as soon as you saw that label?

Place your second file in alphabetical order before or after the first. Continue creating new files depending on what papers you pull out of your Keep pile and add them alphabetically. Don't worry about where to divide the two drawers between A and Z. You will keep placing them in the top drawer until it's full, and then you can begin moving files from the rear of the drawer down to the second drawer.

You may begin to worry that you will quickly run out of files. But you'll soon notice that many of your Keep pile papers are going into files you've already created—for example, another recipe that goes into your "Recipes" file. If you do run out of files, you can always buy some more.

What you do not want to do is save on files by making up vague categories like "Miscellaneous", "Family Papers", or "Business Stuff". If you do that, you'll have an overstuffed folder that's hard to deal with, you'll spend at least 10 minutes going through it to find a single paper, and you won't even be sure in which of the vague categories the paper might be. "Miscellaneous" is *never* the answer to the question, "If I am looking for paper X, will I know it is in this file?"

Of course, if you decide you have been overly specific, you can always combine multiple files into a single one. For example, you might say, "I don't really need separate files for my Toyota and my Honda; one "Cars" file is good enough for both." If this sounds logical to you, then you will be able to find that information when you need it—which is all that matters.

Likewise, don't be afraid to subdivide a category if a folder becomes unwieldy. If you find that your "Recipes" file contains hundreds of recipes, it will be very difficult to find any one particular recipe. So take a few more folders and create a set. You could divide such a folder into "Recipes"—"Appetizers", "Recipes—Main Course", and "Recipes—Desserts", for example.

In practice, you won't have to make too many of these decisions, nor will you find them hard to make when they do come up.

Keep moving. Don't keep reading the papers once you know what they're about. If you realize that something really isn't worth making a file for—*throw it out*. Keep filing until every keeper is filed. Depending on how long you've been letting things go, it may take less than an hour, or several. In any case, it will take less time than you probably think it will, and you'll never have to do it again. In the future, there will be a place for every new paper either in an existing file or in a new file you will make on the spot and put into its slot, in alphabetical order.

The Last Step: Action Items

The action items are the most important and the easiest to manage. Examine each item in the pile as if it were a Must-Do task. Determine if the action deadline is today, tomorrow, or this week and place it in the appropriate desk tray. Is the deadline further away than this week? If so, mark your calendar accordingly and file the paper under an appropriate label so you can pull it out the week that it becomes relevant. If the action that must be taken is a project rather than a single task, break it down into tasks and schedule them accordingly. Repeat this process until all action items have been organized.

That's it. It has probably taken the better part of a day, but now you're set up.

Daily Maintenance

Now that your system is set up, you can turn your attention to its maintenance. In just 10 minutes each day, you can organize your activities into the necessary categories. You can choose to do your planning at the end of the day or the beginning of the day.

Let's say it's Tuesday night and you are planning for Wednesday. Take a look at the three Must-Do lists for Tuesday and use them to make up your new lists for Wednesday. If any "Today" items on the Tuesday list were not finished, they're now overdue. Transfer them to the new "Today" list for Wednesday along with any "Tomorrow" items from the Tuesday list. (Common sense, right?)

Next, check the Tuesday "This Week" list and promote as many items as you can to either the "Today" or "Tomorrow" lists for Wednesday. Last, scan your calendar a few weeks ahead and make sure there isn't anything that needs to be promoted to your "This Week" list.

Your Wednesday lists are now ready. Take one last glance at the "Today" list and make a few notes about scheduling (roughly) the activities on it. Are three items on the list all things that can be done at the same mall? Write MALL next to them. Should one task be done in the morning because it requires unbroken concentration, and your afternoons are usually full of interruptions? Write A.M. next to the task. That level of detail is sufficient—don't try to schedule everything to exact minutes, because it's unrealistic and unnecessary and can be very discouraging when items aren't completed exactly on schedule.

Your lists are now complete. You only have so many Must-Dos for Wednesday, you can see them all at a glance, and you can accomplish them as opportunities arise during the day. It's that simple.

As your day progresses, the world will send you new tasks, appointments, deadlines, pieces of mail, and other paperwork. When this happens, you will know exactly how to keep track of each item so it will be acted upon in time. Your Must-Dos will always get done.

Just Do It

Unless you organize your paperwork and daily tasks, you will not have time to make your dreams of running your own business come true. I know that it's easy to read about a program like this, turn the page, and never actually follow the program. Don't make that mistake.

Making a commitment to getting organized and managing your schedule is the first step toward permanently eliminating a lot of the time-wasting extra work you now have because papers are hard to find, bills are not paid on time, and projects are not completed. Getting organized is the first step toward a life with less stress and guilt, less wasted energy, and more time to do what you really want to do.

You can take that first step in a single day. What are you waiting for?

Understand and Plan Your Finances— Both Personal and Business

One of the scariest things about starting your own business is the idea of doing the financial math. I can certainly relate. I had virtually no background in business accounting and yet wound up crunching numbers for Fortune 500 companies. But as you progress through this chapter, you will hear some good news: to keep the accounts for an average small business, all you need to know are a few simple principles, and all you need to use is an inexpensive software package that is expressly tailored to your needs.

Finances and Me

Math has always been a challenging subject for me. Before I learned that I have dyslexia, I failed the same algebra class five times and continued to struggle with math throughout college. When I first moved out of my parents' house, I found it nearly impossible to balance my checkbook and bounced many checks because of simple math errors. To this day, I still have a problem with transposing numbers.

Maybe it ran in the family. As a child, I often watched my father balance his salon's books. His numbers were always off, and it seemed like there was a new reason why every week. Because he did everything by hand, the records were hard to read and slow to access. Various kinds of important information were never at his fingertips. For example, he was often owed money, but he had no way of quickly finding out who owed him, how much was owed, or when it had been borrowed. Similarly, he'd often have vendors who would promise products or marketing opportunities but no way of tracking who'd promised what. My dad's example taught me that the important thing is not how much you make, but where it goes. I knew there had to be a better way.

Learning on the Job

I started working for Hewlett-Packard (HP) when I was 20 years old. My career at HP began shortly after the company had entered the desktop computer business, so I felt like I was getting into the PC world at the ground floor.

While I was still in high school, I once told my mother of my long-term plan to work there. She said, "Oh, right, you're going to work for a calculator company. Do you really believe everyone wants a *computer* in the house?" I just laughed. Sure enough, she was the first one in the family to ask to use my HP discount for a new computer.

At HP, I soon learned how to use Microsoft Excel. I made up a simple little spreadsheet that would help me with my personal finances by keeping track of all my bills and payments to creditors. Although I had no way of knowing it at the time, I was learning vital skills that would be necessary for my business.

In my financial spreadsheet, I set up a series of tabs for categories like:

- Car—payments, insurance, gas, and maintenance
- Utilities—electricity, phone, and gas
- Household—cleaning supplies, bed linen, etc.
- Grocery—staple foods and beverages
- Dining—lunch, dinner, and snacks outside the home
- Entertainment—movies, school plays, concerts, etc.

This spreadsheet helped me see in a single glance how much money it took to run my household, how much (if any) I could save, how much it would cost me to live if I lost my job, and where I could make cuts in my spending if I had to. It was a simple beginner's tool, but it taught me invaluable lessons.

In Over My Head

When I started Luv's Brownies®, I was also working full-time at Hewlett-Packard (HP), had just started the MBA program at Golden Gate University, and had just learned that the closest person in my life, James, had AIDS and needed intensive medical care. It was the most challenging year of my life, and in the middle of it I took on a new position with greater responsibilities at HP.

I was supposed to be a project manager working with clients' marketing programs. However, I quickly learned that the job was really about crunching numbers. About 80 percent of my time was to be devoted to calculating and tweaking the client's return on investment (ROI) for various marketing activities with a budget between $2 and $6 million.

ROI is an accounting term. It is calculated by determining the net value a particular investment, product, or program earns over a period of time divided by its initial costs. Thus, the higher the ROI, the more worthwhile the program—so you can easily see why HP would want to constantly track the ROI of every marketing program to see which were working and which weren't.

But I was a marketer, not an accountant! With bills to pay, a small business in its infancy, and James to worry about, looking for another job was out of the question. I had to roll with the punches and learn these new skills—fast.

The Balance Sheet

I decided to take an accounting class at the City of San Jose Learning Center. There, I learned a critical lesson I use every day at my bakery business: how to maintain a balance sheet. Fortunately, the basic ideas behind an accounting balance sheet are not that hard to understand.

First, every credit is also a debit. That is, if someone pays you $100, he must deduct $100 from his bank account, so your credit is his debit. The same principle applies to an internal transaction, when the money never leaves your hands. If you take $100 out of your bank account to have cash in your register, the debit from your bank account is equal to the credit in your register. The debit and the credit *balance*, or cancel each other out.

The balance sheet takes this common sense idea a step further. In a business, you have certain assets—your cash on hand, your equipment, other property, and your inventory. But you don't own all of those items free and clear. There are claims against it, such as any debts and obligations you have contracted to pay: your electric bill, the salaries of your employees, or payments on your bank loans, for example. These are called liabilities. When these liabilities are subtracted from your total assets, what's left is what you do own free and clear, which is called your equity or capital.

To restate that mathematically:

Assets – Liabilities = Capital

which is the same as:

Assets = Capital + Liabilities

A balance sheet may be very complicated in detail, but the idea is simple. One side lists all your assets, including the dollar value of each. The other side lists your liabilities and capital. The two sides must always be equal (see Figure 3.1).

A properly maintained balance sheet is a framework for keeping track of where your money really is, where it's going, and how much of it is really yours.

The balance sheet tells you where you stand today; metrics like ROI tell you how your balance sheet will change over time. If your capital is not increasing, or is not increasing quickly enough, you should probably change strategies. Cash flow management and analysis are essential to the success of your business.

Balance sheets are also very useful at tax time, because all busi-

Figure 3.1.

SMITH'S WORLD OF WIDGETS
Balance Sheet for March 31, 2007

Assets		Liabilities	
Cash	$20,000	Owed to bank	$150,000
Stocks	$30,000	Refunds pending	+ $10,000
Factory building	$200,000		
Factory land	$200,000	Total liabilities	$160,000
Equipment	+ $50,000	Owner's equity	+ $340,000
Total assets	$500,000	Liabilities + Equity	$500,000

nesses are legally required to report profits, losses, expenses, and other tax information. The balance sheet organizes this information in a simple and efficient manner.

The Problem of Inventory

Your inventory is the salable parts or products you have on your "shelves" at any given time. I know that inventory doesn't necessarily sound like a problem—after all, you need to have products in order to sell them—but it is. Inventory ties up your cash and takes up valuable space. Excess stock can be damaged or stolen. Products or parts can degrade in quality while in storage. Last, inventory is usually taxable as well.

So you want to keep inventory to a minimum, and that means being able to locate it and move it out as quickly as possible. This leads the discussion to three concepts: just-in time (JIT); first in, first out (FIFO); and last in, first out (LIFO).

- *JIT.* In the old days, most companies had to keep a large stock of goods on hand so they wouldn't find themselves out of a particular item. However, with faster communications and transportation and computers to track and make more accurate predictions of supply and demand, more and more companies can keep an absolute minimum of inventory and have products ready "just in time" to ship out—with only a small reserve remaining on the shelf. Jeff Bezos's Amazon.com is a prime example of a JIT business.

- *FIFO*. This system of inventory flow is particularly well-suited to perishable products. Suppose you're selling milk in a grocery store. You'll want to sell the oldest milk first, so you're always moving it from the back of the store to the front row of the milk racks. Thus, the first milk inventory that you received is the first you wish to sell.

- *LIFO*. Suppose you have a lot of heavy and identical hardware items that aren't perishable at all. It's a waste of effort to rotate them; it makes more sense to sell the ones you just bought if they're more convenient to reach. LIFO is sometimes a better choice for tax purposes, too. If you bought 50 widgets for $1.00 apiece and more recently bought another 50 widgets of the same kind for $1.50 apiece, and you can subsequently sell 50 widgets for $2.00, selling the last-in 50 means a lower declared profit, lower tax on the income, and a lower value for the remaining inventory if it is taxed.

With some products (such as the fresh milk in the first example), common sense will dictate whether FIFO or LIFO is the way to go. With other products, you may have to experiment to see which system of arranging your inventory saves you time, effort, or taxes—but it's worth doing.

Inventory control means knowing everything you have, and knowing exactly where it is. If you can't put your hands on a product or part when you need it, it's worthless. It's not just failing to make money—it's also costing you the expense of storing it.

In addition to tracking the location of your inventory, you must also constantly update its real value. Most goods—perishable and nonperishable alike—lose value over time.

I saw a disastrous example once while consulting at a Silicon Valley software company. The company kept a stock of Internet-connection cables that automatically retracted into easy-to-pack little balls as promotional giveaways for its customers with laptops. It was a great gift—back in the dial-up Internet era. Now, of course, laptops usually come with wireless Internet capacity and rarely need these cables. The company had moved on to more contemporary promotional gifts, but it didn't realize that the old ones were still in inventory. Before management caught on, the company had paid $8,000 a year in storage costs for four years to keep old merchandise that no one wanted anymore—a total loss of $32,000, not including what it had paid for the cables in the first place!

What Mama Kake Taught Me

The value of a cash-flow statement. I was learning valuable lessons at work. But a lesson doesn't hit home until it applies to you personally. Even though I was calculating ROIs day after day at HP, I didn't immediately see how these fundamentals of accounting applied to my own business.

When I first started my bakery, I rented bakery space, attended school, and still worked my day job at HP. I spent most holidays baking, wrapping and delivering, and missed out on Fourth of July celebrations, barbecues, concerts, and myriad other activities. I remember waking up at 3 a.m. to bake, wrap, and deliver brownies, and then reporting to work at HP at 8 a.m. I'd be at the office until 5 or 6 p.m. By the time I got home, I was exhausted. Sometimes I'd be up for 24 hours straight—baking all night and then going to work at 8 a.m. I've never had a romantic Valentine's Day in my life. For the first few years of the bakery, I just wanted to give it all up and have a normal life.

Everyone I knew told me to quit my job and open a storefront at a mall. But my mentor, Mama Kake, told me not to quit my day job and not to open a retail location. She had rented her bakery by the hour to a number of other businesses, and for one reason or another, none of them had gone on to open a storefront. To explain why, she showed me her own income statement. Figure 3.2 shows a simplified version with fabricated sums.

Figure 3.2.

KATHY'S KREATIVE KAKES
1/1/1997–12/31/1997

Sales	$582,000
Cost of sales	($300,000)
Operating expenses	+ ($130,000)
Earnings	$152,000

After Mama Kake explained her finances and the overhead costs of her bakery and staff, I realized that the money I was making would be gobbled up as fast as my brownies. Mama Kake asked me to prepare my own cash-flow statement, which is shown in Figure 3.3.

Figure 3.3.

LUV'S BROWNIES
1/1/1997–12/31/1997

Sales	$20,000
Cost of sales	($90,000)
Operating expenses	+ ($20,000)
Loss	($90,000)
Reserve cash in the bank	+ $60,000
Deficit	($30,000)

That's right, *negative* $30,000! The last thing I needed to do was take on new overhead.

Before you start your business, do the math. Those who had advised me to open a storefront, keep more inventory, and hire a staff to carry some of the burden didn't understand the expenses and the overhead that these things would entail.

Break-even analysis. After setting me straight on the fundamentals, Kathy next made me realize the importance of a break-even analysis. A break-even analysis has three components:

- *Break-even volume.* This is the number of units of product that must be sold just to cover costs, or break even. It is what the break-even analysis attempts to uncover: your minimum sales goal.
- *Fixed costs.* Fixed costs are constant expenses—rent, insurance, and other unchanging overhead.
- *The per-unit net income (also known as the contribution margin).* This is the price charged per unit of product minus the variable costs of production. This is the price charged per unit of product minus the variable costs of production. If your costs to produce a cake are $2 worth of ingredients and $7 worth of labor, and you sell it for $11, then your per unit net income is $11 minus ($2 + $7), or $2.

Thus, the formula is:

Break-even volume = Fixed costs ÷ Per-unit net

For example, one of my consulting arrangements required me to figure out the break-even point for all the software that the company needed to sell for a certain period. The company sold only one product, which made the process easier. The software sold for $20. The company incurred a $5 variable cost for each unit that was sold, so the per-unit net was $15. The company's fixed cost for the projected period was $110,000. So, the break-even formula revealed:

110,000 ÷ 15 = 7,333

Therefore, to break even, the company had to sell at least 7,333 units. It now knew its goal.

The same formula applies even to a little business selling brownies. When I knew how many brownies I had to sell a month to break even, I could begin to evaluate whether or not I should exhibit at certain bridal or gift fairs. If a certain fair would take up a tenth of my selling time for the month, the smallest number of brownies I would want to sell there would be a tenth of my monthly break-even amount. So, I'd ask the event's organizers how many visitors were expected to attend the fair, and then I would walk the show, looking at my place in the layout and making an educated guess at how much of the foot traffic would pass my booth. If the number of potential customers suggested I could make more than my break-even goal, I knew it was worth doing; otherwise, I needed to make better use of my time.

Doing a break-even analysis also gives you a handle on other useful numbers. Once I decide that a certain fair is worthwhile because 200 people will pass my booth a day, I know I need to have at least 200 business cards available a day, or perhaps 500 for the weekend. (However, because of the pricing structure for cards, I would never order fewer than 1,000 at one time.) I also know how many brownie samples to bring: 200 people means 400 samples, because nobody takes just one. But I'm always prepared to change my estimates on the basis of experience.

For one month's bridal fairs, for instance, I decided to bake my brownies on-site as a quality-control measure. I found that the smell of hot, fresh brownies brought me a larger percentage of the show's total foot traffic than I had ever received before. The numbers had changed, so I quickly changed the number of brownies I expected to turn out every day and reaped a big increase in profits. And you can bet that if I possibly can, I bake on-site at fairs.

It's always about the numbers. If you don't know the numbers, you don't know what you're doing, and you can't plan for the future.

And Now, the Good News

As I promised at the beginning of this chapter, you don't need an accounting degree to stay on top of the numbers. There are accounting software programs designed specifically for small businesses.

With programs like Intuit's QuickBooks, you can keep a balance sheet, budget, pay bills, control inventory, and make forecasts of your future needs. It includes balance sheet, invoice, and statement templates, and you can even print your own checks. It will calculate reports on inventory, profit and loss, accounts receivable, accounts payable, or your taxes. All you have to do is fill in the blanks, which primarily involves logging what comes in and what goes out.

I like QuickBooks, but there are several other programs with comparable features, and if one of them seems to offer an advantage to you, go for it. But find a program and use it. And if that means you have to buy a computer first, the time you'll save and the accuracy of the results will be well worth it.

Staying on Top of the Numbers

Once you've selected a financial software program, always follow these rules.

Review your balance sheet, budget, and cash flow before making any financial decision. I know sometimes it's hard to resist the temptation to buy what you want when you want it, but remember that your wants are endless. Think instead about what you and your business really need. If you can't afford it, don't do it.

Have a plan and budget for at least one year ahead. Be sure to include marketing and promotional costs. Remember that it's all one integrated business—production, promotion, marketing, and sales.

For future planning, always do a break-even analysis. It's easy to think, "I'm making a profit anytime and anywhere I sell my product." But that's only a profit per unit. If you're not selling enough volume to cover your fixed overhead, you're still losing money. Doing a break-even analysis beforehand helps you find high-volume venues and avoid wasting your time and energy elsewhere.

Learn from your competition. Before I started Luv's, I did extensive research on the cookie empires of Famous Amos and Mrs. Fields to understand how those companies had grown. When you're starting your business, you may have trouble estimating what costs and prices you will be dealing with.

See what other players in your field are doing. Sometimes you can ally with what might seem to be to be a competing firm. Even though we're competitors for the Valentine's Day and wedding trade, my mentor Mama Kake helped me put together my business plan, offered great advice and trades, rented her kitchen to me, and shared her practical knowledge. As long as you're not setting up shop directly across the street, some competitors will be happy to share information with you.

Minimize inventory as much as you can. Make sure you know—unit by unit—what you have and where it is, and keep that information handy, so it is accessible with the least amount of trouble. Move your inventory out before it loses value.

Make a monthly review of your accounts receivable. One month, I was shocked to realize that I was flat broke. I'd been so busy filling orders that I didn't realize that a lot of my customers owed me money.

One customer had placed an order for 25 Christmas gift baskets and party trays. He owed me more than $4,500. When I tried to collect, he had a million excuses for me. But once his debt had been overdue for more than 90 days, I reported him to a collection agency—and he paid me cash the next day. Many companies initiate the collection process at 60 days past due.

Remember that it is always wise to warn the customer before sending him or her to a collection agency. That's usually enough to get payment. If a collection agency is successful, it keeps 50 percent of the recovered debt. If you warn the customer beforehand, you get to keep all of the recovered debt.

Today, I never move forward with an order unless I have a valid credit card number on file.

Keep up with your cash transactions. Get a receipt for everything you purchase and drop it in a big manila envelope or shoebox at the end of the day. Once a week, clear out the envelope and enter the information into your accounts. If you don't follow this simple procedure, cash will disappear, and you won't know whether the expense was personal or a deductible business expense. Your business software will figure the deductions for you—all you have to do is spend 5 or 10 minutes a week entering the data. You're throwing money away if you don't record these transactions.

Hire a tax attorney. My tax attorney provides extensive professional guidance, and he has gently put a stop to a lot of ideas that were best left as daydreams. A good tax attorney has seen businesses of many different kinds from the bottom line up; it's hard to find a better adviser.

Follow these simple steps, and you should remain in control. Keeping good books, and making plans based on them, means running your business instead of letting your business run you.

Start Small and Create a Solid Business Plan Around Something You Love

Your Business Isn't a Building

If you want to own your own business, you probably have a vivid mental picture of it. It may be a personal little shop or a huge display center, with plenty of exciting products displayed on shelves. And of course, you see yourself in a big office, with a mahogany desk and a spectacular view that will impress all your visitors.

Well, get over it.

Your business is not a building. It is *you*, your ideas and energy, your talents and abilities, and your processes for making or selling products. That brick-and-mortar store has a mortgage and a whopping property tax attached to it. Unless you absolutely need it, you don't want it.

Don't own. Rent space, and don't rent space full-time if you can rent it part-time. Don't rent space at all if you can get by at home with a phone and an Internet-based "virtual office."

For many start-up businesses—and you might as well begin thinking of yourself as a start-up now, because if you plan to start your own business, that's what you are—getting by without owning a store or office can be the difference between profitability and going broke.

Own the Business, Not the Bakery

In 1996, I realized rent and other building-related overhead could drag my business under. I decided to find a bakery that would allow me to pay by the hour to use its facilities. Since I was just getting my business off the ground and training new contract employees, I had to make sure rent wasn't going to kill my profits.

Minimizing overhead. Unlike paying rent for a building space, where I would have to pay every month, no matter what, the business model of baking by the hour gave me the flexibility of using space—and paying for it—only when I had orders in hand. This was a win-win strategy for the owner of the bakery and for my business. My team would use the licensed kitchen facilities during the evening or early-morning hours, when the bakery wasn't normally operational. The bakery owner would be earning money during those hours. I would receive a little more knowledge of how someone else's bakery was run, and could use that experience to build my own business processes.

The business model for baking has changed radically. Costco, Safeway, Wal-Mart, and other large grocery stores are capturing the market for fresh goods baked from scratch on the premises. With their heavy foot traffic, in-store coupons, and customer loyalty programs, these retailers can count on a certain level of sales year-round. Because of economies of scale, the big stores can offer low prices and stay open longer hours and on weekends. It's hard for small bakeries to compete.

You may have noticed that in newer grocery stores, the entry doors are usually situated near either the flowers and fresh fruit or the baked-goods and prepared-food sections. The prepared-food sections are growing steadily, because people are busier, are working longer hours, and have less time to cook. The frozen and canned-food sections are shrinking. Grocery stores are cashing in on what they can prepare on the premises, and bakery items are a big profit center.

Maximizing channel partners. The products you don't sell directly to customers have to reach them through some other channel. A dealer or distributor that carries your goods is called a "channel partner," and it usually gets a price discount for its help with distribution, advertising, and marketing. (The terms *channel* and *channel partner* are often used interchangeably.)

When I first started my business, I had a lot of grocery stores as channel partners. Every Monday and Wednesday I would get up at 2 a.m., go the bakery, bake 200 to 500 brownies, and deliver them to two grocery store chains by 6 a.m. Then I would go running at the park, go home, take a shower, get dressed, and go to work at HP. The effort was well worth it, because I had a steady stream of payments coming in all the time. It was a wholesale business—not high profit—but I could count on it, and it was a nice chunk of change to have every 15 days.

The grocery stores sealed the brownies and sold them as their own brand. As time went on, the grocery stores began placing direct orders with me for their customers. I was only getting paid wholesale for this steady stream of orders as well, but soon the stores were also relaying requests that customers wanted me to bake for their private parties, which was very lucrative. It was a good arrangement for me.

When I was selling in grocery stores, I would always look for ways to build foot traffic. I sent direct-mail pieces to particular zip codes, offered print ad specials, sent bulk e-mails to my San Francisco customer base, and so forth. For Valentine's Day, Mother's Day, and Father's Day, I would do in-store baking demonstrations, sign books, and hand out free bite-sized brownies.

After about four years of these arrangements, both grocery stores told me they had decided to bake brownies in their stores from scratch. It was a tremendous blow to my business. But soon, they let me know that their own brownies weren't selling as well as mine had, and both stores decided to bring me back as a guest baker for seasonal stints. Today, it's a smaller part of my business than it used to be, but I'm lucky: many local florists and bakeries have been completely wiped out by competition from grocery stores.

For instance, Mama Kake has told me that since many prospective brides and grooms are looking for ways to cut costs, they often see the wedding cake as an easy target. They might order a pretty cake for the core wedding party at a traditional bakery and feed the rest of the guests grocery or big-box retailer cake. Their attitude is, "Let them eat Costco."

Effects on suppliers. This sort of scaling back and restructuring is happening at every level of the baking business. I went to my local bakery supply one day back in 2000 to purchase some Guittard chocolate. The company, which had appeared to be thriving a week before, was packed up. The owner told me, "We are closing our doors. Smaller bakeries are going to Costco to buy their flour and sugar. With the loss of their business, the larger suppliers are staying in business by buying up the smaller suppliers and consolidating." Within months of that conversation, I could find only two or three bakery suppliers left in the San Francisco Bay Area—all surviving off high volume alone.

Larger suppliers only cater to larger bakeries. The minimum order requirements would drive my little "Luv Shack" under. Fortunately, Mama Kake had an existing relationship with all of the larger suppliers and allowed me to fold my orders in with hers. Of course, I and the other smaller bakeries could also fall back on Costco for the staple commodities—butter, flour, and sugar.

The perils of a storefront. Over the next few years, rental, lease, and purchase prices of commercial property fell. I sometimes considered opening my own storefront bakery. But you don't just learn from the experience of those who succeed—you also learn from those who fail. I am always checking out the competition—particularly bakeries with a narrow specialty like my own.

One of the most impressive shops I ever saw was a brand-new storefront bakery in the heart of Silicon Valley's upscale customer base. This store specialized in cheesecakes—the best you'd ever had, in 20 different varieties. It went broke within two years. Meanwhile, I hang on, because I continue to bake by the hour—making use of existing capital equipment and infrastructure without the overhead of owning it.

Of course, I might still want to open my own storefront someday. A good example of slow and steady growth is Harry and David, a retailer of fresh fruit, candy, nuts, appetizers, desserts, and flowers.

The company was a local Oregon orchard in the 1900s that expanded into the mail-order business in the 1930s with a Fruit-of-the-Month Club. Only in recent years has the company opened outlets in malls and shopping centers. Like Harry and David, I'm prepared to wait until the time is right for my own storefront—when the numbers add up.

Bigger Isn't Necessarily Better

One way new businesses get trapped into taking on too much overhead is by trying to grow too fast.

Startups in the San Francisco Bay Area always seemed to think they should grow at an exponential rate. But booms tend to be followed by busts. There's nothing more flattering than having venture capitalists tell you that they want to give you the money to help your company grow. The trouble is, they are generally looking for you to grow in whatever direction they think will offer the quickest return on their investment, and sometimes their notions are completely unrealistic.

For example, some potential investors hoped I could sell Luv's Brownies® worldwide. It sounded wonderful, and the numbers looked good on paper. But in the real world, it's not so easy to get a perishable item out of the United States and all the way to Singapore before it's inedible. Perishable products have a shelf life of three to five days. I have explored the idea of using preservatives to extend that timeframe, but they dramatically change the taste and texture of the brownies. I won't jeopardize quality, so further research and development are needed.

During the big start-up boom of the late 1990s, the phrase "We are growing" meant different things to different people. To me, growing my business meant getting more customer orders, broadening my markets, and continuously having feet on the street to sell brownies. To a lot of start-ups, growing meant leasing vast tracts of office space and recruiting armies of employees. Many measured their success in buildings, not in business—with often disastrous consequences.

The Right Way to Grow

Amazon.com is one of the great success stories of the Internet era. Its founder, Jeff Bezos, initiated a business that is tough to make profitable even at a good storefront location—retailing books—and created an online version that is healthy, diversified, and profitable today.

For years, many business analysts cast dire predictions every quarter that Amazon was a year away from failure. Like most start-ups, Amazon lost tremendous amounts of money as it built its customer base. And what the analysts could see was this: despite all of Bezos's revolutionary successes in advertising, merchandising, and taking orders online, he had one big liability—in order to supply super-fast order fulfillment, he had to have a lot of books ready to ship in a brick-and-mortar warehouse. Clearly, the analysts said, the bigger Amazon gets, the longer its product list will be. The warehouses will have to be large and peppered around the country, and expensive full-time employees will be working in those mighty warehouses. Sooner or later, they speculated, these transaction costs would drag down his business and sink it.

The analysts were right, but they were also wrong. They were right that Amazon could not succeed if it became the biggest brick-and-mortar bookstore in the world. They were wrong because Bezos was too smart to fall into that trap.

Thinking of buying a book? Visit Amazon.com. Type the name of the book into the site's search engine. You'll probably be given a choice of buying the book new and buying it used. If you want to buy it new, you may notice there's a little line in the book's description telling you that Amazon has only a few copies left, but more are on the way. How can the biggest bookstore in the world have only a few copies of the book? Because its computers have indicated that a few is all it needs in the warehouse this week, and it will order more next week. For new books, Bezos uses computing power to follow a just-in-time (JIT) strategy that keeps his warehouses at reasonable and manageable sizes.

Suppose you order the book used instead of new. You'd pay a lot less for a used book. You might think this would be a bad deal for Amazon, but in reality the opposite is true. Amazon often makes more money on sales of used books than it does on sales of new books.

If you use Amazon to purchase a used book, the company passes your order on to one of several thousand used-book businesses around the country. Amazon takes a significant cut of the sale price and charges a fee for handling the transaction, and the used-book store that warehouses the book sends it to you and deals with any customer service problems that may arise.

Amazon brokers the selling of used books and allows individuals and small businesses to sell almost any other product you can think of in its Amazon Marketplace. These virtual shops work in a very similar way: the customer finds the product via the Amazon website, orders it through Amazon, and Amazon passes the order on and takes a cut of the transaction and assesses its fees.

In 2002, Amazon posted its first profitable quarter, and the critics were silenced. Why? Because Jeff Bezos realized that his business isn't a building that warehouses books; it's actually a business *model* for advertising, merchandising, and taking orders online. It's a set of *repeatable processes* that can be applied to any product—not just books.

I've gone into the Amazon example in great detail because you might want to consider structuring your own small business as a virtual shop in Amazon Marketplace or as a similar arrangement with a different established Web presence. Yes, Amazon takes a cut of transactions in your Marketplace shop—but it's a win-win proposition, because you get access to the millions of customers who visit the Amazon website every day. Keep that possibility in mind. I buy bakery hours from an established brick-and-mortar bakery, and you can take advantage of an established Internet marketing infrastructure.

Grow the right way, not the wrong way.

You Don't Need to Rent an Office

To minimize my operational costs, I decided to turn my living room into an office. I sold or donated most of my furniture and purchased an ergonomic desk and chair and file cabinets.

Admittedly, you think twice about having company over when your living room is crammed with a love seat, a 19-inch television from my high school days, a huge desk, and file cabinets. But it worked for me. Later, I decided to go all the way—I gave my kitchen table to my father and turned my kitchen into a gift basket assembly line.

At first, I used my apartment address and home phone number for everything. It was cheap and easy. As time went on, however, I started to get strange messages on the Brownie Hotline. Men I didn't know would drive by my apartment and leave me phone messages like, "I know you're home. Why aren't you answering the phone?" Another hassle was receiving packages and signing for Fed Ex or UPS shipments—I couldn't be at home all day.

To avoid these hassles, I decided to use a mailing facility (such as a UPS Store). For less than $40 a month, you can receive all the following services:

- Someone at the office address seven days a week
- Someone to sign for packages
- An official FedEx drop-off and pick-up location
- A physical address that customers can use to pick up items such as Valentine's Day gift baskets or wedding favors
- Copy and print services
- Computer services
- 24-hour access to mailbox services
- Faxing and receiving
- The ability to call in and check for mail or packages
- Complete access to packaging supplies, and even the option of having an employee package products and ship them

You'll get all these services—plus the huge advantage of *not owning the building*. If your business fails, or you have to move, you can get rid of your virtual office with one phone call. There's no capital equipment to sell, and no lease to escape.

You Don't Need a Big Inventory

In every business course I have ever taken, inventory is identified as a nightmare for many companies. It takes up space, adds to the building overhead you're trying to eliminate, and may be subject to taxation. Although it is a chore to keep inventory to a minimum, it's worth it.

Of course, you always start off small. Originally, I stored all of my gift baskets, tins, shipping boxes, and packaging supplies on my apartment terrace. I always knew exactly what I had and what I needed to order. But as you grow, this option won't always be possible. You can buy inexpensive PC software that will monitor how much inventory you have in stock and what it's costing you as you hold it.

But remember, you still have to manage inventory, and JIT processes—constant monitoring to keep supplies, output, and orders in balance—are the key. You'll also need to locate long-term and short-term suppliers for your business.

Long-term suppliers. Long-term suppliers are the suppliers you will use for large orders. I call them "long-term" because they generally require longer lead times for orders. In return, you generally pay less for the supplies. Long-term suppliers are an excellent option for preparing for a peak season.

Suppose I have a box supplier who charges $0.35 per box, but to get that price, I must buy a minimum quantity of 1,000 and wait three weeks for delivery. My out-of-pocket expense would be $350 plus delivery charges and travel time. But for Valentine's Day, I know I will have enough orders to use that many boxes.

Short-term suppliers. During slower periods, if I only need 10 or 15 boxes, I'd use a short-term supplier. That's a distributor who sells boxes by the piece and not in bulk. Ten boxes for $1.95 each means my out-of-pocket expense would be $19.50 plus travel time and expenses to pick up the boxes. The upside: I won't have 990 extra boxes gathering dust and tax obligations.

This JIT planning makes my tax attorney and accountant happy. I don't have to tie my money up in inventory; instead, I can divert my available funds to marketing and increasing sales. I'm not putting together a plant, a workforce, or an inventory. I'm putting together a set of processes that may someday be a turnkey franchise I can hand off to others.

Your Business Isn't Your Business

I hope I've convinced you that your business isn't a building. Next, I'm going to tell you something even more surprising—*your business isn't your business*. What could I possibly mean by that? If your business isn't your business—what is it? Let me give you some examples.

McDonald's Isn't in the Burger Business

Most people think McDonald's is a fast-food business—after all, it sells burgers, fries, and salads. However, this fast-food giant doesn't make its biggest profits on food. Consider the myriad costs involved: advertising, building overhead, employee costs, raw food, transportation and spoilage, energy and water, and packaging, to name a few. When you consider the low prices of McDonald's food, it's amazing there's any profit at all!

Now consider how much money McDonald's makes on the product that requires the least output, labor, and maintenance: soft drinks. A soda can cost up to $2 at a fast-food restaurant, but it costs pennies to serve—including the cup.

The fast-food business is not the business it appears to be on the surface. It's the soda business, and movie theaters are in it, too.

The So-called Movie Business

Movie theater managers have a tremendous problem. In theory, their business is selling movie tickets. However, history has proven that people have more sales resistance to increases in movie ticket prices than for other goods. Think about it. There's always considerable grumbling about the high cost of going to the movies, but the truth is that ticket prices have increased less in the past 50 years than many things you can name.

Of course, it's hard to compare apples with oranges. Since 1960, basic food commodities like milk and eggs have gone up very little in price, while undergraduate tuition at Harvard has gone from $1,350 to more than *$33,000* in 2007. But consider some entertainment items that are somewhat comparable to a movie ticket. Paperback books that cost $0.35 in 1960 are at least $7.00 today; comic books that cost $0.10 are $3.00 today. How much have movie tickets gone up?

By 2005 (the last year for which reliable figures are available from the National Association of Theater Owners), you could pay $10.00 for an evening show in America's largest cities, but the *average* cost per ticket, when you figured in the discount prices for matinees, children and seniors, was $6.41. The average cost in 1960 was about $0.75. So while paperbacks have gone up 20 times and comic books 30 times, movie tickets have gone up less than 10 times. They aren't leading the inflationary pack—not even close.

But it doesn't feel that way to consumers. Who knows why? Maybe it's because we all associate going to the movies with being a kid and remember the ticket prices from when we were a kid each time we pass the ticket counter. Theater owners have learned they just can't raise ticket prices as often or as much as other businesses can reprice their goods.

And they can't ask for a bigger cut of the profits from the movie studios. Today, movie studios are realizing that *they aren't in the movie business either*; increasingly, they are in the DVD and spin-off merchandising business. In reality, they really don't care if the movie theaters slowly die off; thus, they will not give the theaters a bigger cut of the ticket price.

So where do theater managers make up the difference? The snack counter, of course. Snacks are their real business—candy, soda, bottled water, and popcorn.

Popcorn is as big a moneymaker as soda. Another benefit: salty movie popcorn pumps up the soda and bottled-water sales. According to investigative reporter Edward Jay Epstein, movie popcorn yields $0.90 of profit on every $1.00 in sales. A theater's profit on ticket sales is a fraction of that.

The Gas Station

Everyone likes to complain about the price of gasoline, which is directly related to the price of oil. But there's a big difference between owning an oil well and owning a gas station.

Like the theater owner, a gas station owner is at the mercy of his suppliers—and he faces much more competition. In fact, his share of the gas price is low, and he's lucky if he makes $50,000 a year in profits on gas. To pay his expenses and make real profits, he must sell other items to the many customers who come to him for gas—items such as new wiper blades, car washes, oil changes, hot dogs, candy, and—you guessed it—soda.

Since the invention of self-serve gas pumps that take ATM and credit cards, the gas station managers now have to work a little harder to get you into the store or up-sell you in some other way. That's why more and more of them are combining their stores with a Subway or other fast-food franchise, or adding car wash facilities and offering a discount on the price of gas with the purchase of a car wash.

By now I'm sure you get the idea. The real business of the fast-food business is soda; the real business of the movie theater business is popcorn; and to bring it full circle, the real business of the gas station is fast food.

Once I came to understand this principle, I began to think about what business I was in. What businesses *could* I be in?

Applying the Lesson to Luv's

Most bakeries are labor intensive. If baked goods are your only product, they can quickly tie up all your time, effort, and energy—and where are you going to grow from there?

I'd often help out at Mama Kake's bakery on major holidays like Valentine's Day and Mother's Day. Many customers would rush in

*Seasonal packages include roses, balloons, and gift
baskets filled with Luv's decadent heart-shaped wonders.*

to pick up a cake or gift basket and use the bakery's telephone to order flowers or balloons—sometimes from two different places. That meant that these customers would have to make a second and perhaps a third trip before rushing home to deliver the goodies.

A little research revealed that a wholesale florist sells roses to retailers for $0.50 to $1.25 each. The wholesaler sells prearranged flowers for $10.00 to $25.00 that can be retailed for $45.00 to $105.00. Balloons are sold with a similarly large retail markup.

I thought about the potential for my business. Many of my customers were trying to create sentimental celebrations. What more could they ask for than roses, balloons, and brownies shaped like hearts? And what if they could get them all in one place? I decided to offer a one-stop shop.

After I'd sold flowers and balloons alongside my brownies for about a year, I totaled the numbers. I was amazed. I couldn't believe I had made thousands of dollars just on roses and balloons. On Mother's Day and Valentine's Day, I'm a florist and a bakery.

My business started out selling a basic, one-size brownie for all occasions. It's turned into three product lines (heart-shaped brownie cakes, mail-order gifts, and wedding favors) and multiple categories within those product lines (different sizes of cake, special gift baskets, and wedding favors.) Different products are cash cows at different times, depending on the season. My business is whatever business my customer is looking to spend on for that particular day.

Applying the Lesson to Your Business

Here are three guidelines to follow:

1. *Don't limit your notion of what your business is, but keep taking a fresh look around for other possibilities.* From the early 1900s until the 1970s, the average American who shaved used the same metal-handled razor every day, carefully ejecting disposable "safety" blades and injecting new ones into the razor head as needed.

Then in the 1970s, someone came up with the idea of idea of a disposable razor that was primarily made of plastic and contained miniature blades. It would be so cheap that the user could just throw it away and buy another for a cost comparable to buying replacement safety blades alone.

You know what the reaction of the big U.S. razor manufacturers was? *That isn't our business.* "We make a sturdy, elegant razor that the customer uses for years, and we supply the customer with blades. Disposables are cheap and ugly and only of interest to travelers who forgot to pack their real razors." That's not a direct quote, but it accurately describes the attitude; the razor manufacturers couldn't see disposable razors as part of their business.

Meanwhile, another company looked at the same potential product. The French company Bic had historically specialized in ballpoint pens and cigarette lighters. But Bic's management didn't say, "This is not our business. We make ballpoint pens and cigarette lighters. We don't know anything about razors." No. They took a step back and saw the big picture. They said, "We make disposable pens and disposable lighters—some people buy one fancy pen or lighter and refill it for years, but millions prefer the convenience of a disposable. A disposable pen is just a plastic gizmo with a little metal in it; these razors are the same thing, only easier to make. *Of course this is our business!*"

The result? Bic jumped in and made the product, which soon attracted a huge market: 70 percent of the people who use non-electric shavers. The old-time razor manufacturers got a late start, and it took them years and years of lost money before they got a share of the market.

Don't tell yourself what business you're in—*ask* yourself what business you *could* be in.

2. Look for logical connections or complementary ideas that work with your original business idea. Sometimes the connections are easy to find. If you serve food, you'll serve drinks, too. People who pull into a gas station are often traveling a long distance and have been waiting for miles and miles to use the bathroom and pick up a snack. Everyone likes to eat and drink during a movie.

But don't forget to step back and see the fuzzier connections. (Think of that old game show *Pyramid.*) Brownies and flowers and balloons don't seem to have much in common, but they are connected by a larger idea: "Things you might take to a party or celebration." Razors and pens and lighters don't seem to have much in common, but they are connected by a larger idea: "Disposable products you could make out of similar materials on similar production lines."

Some country stores have made a lot of money selling products with no connection except "stuff our customers want on a Saturday night"—though personally, I always get a little nervous when I see the sign, "GAS - LIQUOR - AMMO!"

3. Look for a product or service with a high profit margin and low labor and maintenance costs. If a new line doesn't pay for itself at least as well as what you already carry, why shift your attention to it? A customer has to be willing to pay the markup on the new item, or there's no point in offering it. The usual reason a customer will pay an unusually high markup is for convenience. It's often worth it to a customer to pay more for an item on the spot versus going elsewhere, waiting in line, and paying less (or, in the Internet era, purchasing an item online for less and waiting a while for it to arrive). Successful corner stores that operate 24 hours a day aren't called "limited-selection stores" or "high-priced stores"—although these names would be accurate. They're called convenience stores for a reason. Look for ways that you can sell convenience.

My greatest achievement of this kind was to sell bottled water at my brownie concessions at art and wine festivals in the San Francisco Bay area. I often found that customers who would purchase brownie sundaes at the concessions would ask for water afterward. For one festival, I bought 5,000 bottles at $0.13 cents each and sold them all for $1.00 each—a profit of $4,350.00 on nothing but water.

Traps to Avoid

1. Don't add a new product line just to attract new business. Always run the numbers and make sure the new business is paying for itself.

Imagine you own a convenience store. You might consider renting a pinball or video game machine for your store, thinking it will draw in kids who will put money into the machine and buy snacks from you. Maybe they will. But think about the potential downsides. What if they frequently shoplift? What if they tie up your counter staff with requests for quarters or complaints about the machine? What if they loiter at your business for hours on end and scare away other customers? If these things happen, your share of the quarters isn't going to be enough to make the games worthwhile. The new business won't pay for itself.

Now, let's flip that example. Let's say that you or a partner of yours knows how to repair pinball and video games. If that's the case, then you can purchase and refurbish some old games and own them outright, and all the quarters will go to you. You could change your convenience store into an arcade and make space for the games by giving up most of your old product lines and selling only high-profit sodas, candy, and snacks that appeal to your new customer base. You'll lose your older customers, but you won't be carrying the overhead of all the lower-profit products they used to buy. You'd be making more money than ever before.

What's the difference between the two cases? The second version is a good business all by itself; you've structured it to pay its own way instead of just being a means to drag a few extra people into a store.

2. Don't change business models without testing the product first. Would adding video games at your store, nail care at your hair salon, or ice cream at your bakery pay its own way or not? Even if the numbers look good on paper, the only way you can find out for sure is to test before you make a commitment. Rent the equipment for a few months before buying it to make sure the customers will be there. Common sense? Sure. But you'd be amazed how many small businesses go broke trying to expand in the wrong direction, when a little testing would have told them not to go there.

3. Don't shift into a business you can't love. The bottom line is important. If the business you love won't make money, you can't keep it. But that doesn't mean you have to take on a business you don't like just because it's more profitable.

A mom-and-pop sewing shop might make a lot more money as an adult book and video store, but if you wouldn't be happy working in that environment and with those customers, perhaps you should wait for a better idea to come along. As an entrepreneur, you are likely to put more hours into your new business than you will spend with your family or in any other aspect of your life. If you can't find any enjoyment in that time, there's no point to it. In the long run, it won't even be profitable—you can't keep coming up with the best product for your customers if you don't respect that product and those customers. Don't just chase the money. When you work toward your dream and love what you do, things fall into place and the money will follow.

Don't be afraid to stick with your own interests and enthusiasms. The fact that you know more and care more about a particular field than most people is going to give you an edge. Just make sure the numbers are there, too. If it pays its own way, and you love it—*that's* your business.

Your Business Is What You Plan

You Don't Know Your Business Without a Plan

What should your business be? The best way to figure that out is to write a business and marketing plan. A well-written business plan is a road map to where you want to go. It's also a living document that constantly changes to deal with new ideas, new conditions, and new customer needs. I can't even count how many times I've changed my plan.

For instance, in 2000 I planned to open a storefront bakery at a new shopping center. If you've read this far, you know why I didn't. But until you make a plan and have real numbers on paper to look at, how can you make a solid judgment about whether it will work or not?

Below is a list of questions to think about before writing your plan. Be sure that you address all of the questions before beginning to write. Your original version doesn't have to be perfect, but before you can change your course, you have to *set* a course.

Building a Business Plan, Step by Step

Part 1: Your Product/Service

- What products or services do you provide?
- How many days a week will you be open for business?
- How does your product differ from similar products on the market?

Part 2: Your Market

- To whom will you sell? Channels (vendors, like grocery stores or retailers)? Distributors? The public?
- Do you have an existing customer base?
- What kinds of lifestyles do they lead?
- Do you know the average age of your customers?
- Do you know the average income level of your customers?

- Are most of your customers single? Married? Employed? Retired?
- How much money do you expect your average customer to spend with your business each year?

Considering all the factors listed, why would these customers want to buy your product or service?

Part 3: Your Location

- Where will your business be headquartered?
- Where will your point-of-sale location be (if different)?
- Is your point-of-sale location easily and conveniently accessible by public transportation? By car? Does the area have heavy foot traffic? Is it located near a freeway (i.e., near an exit)?
- Is ample parking available for customers and employees?
- Are the nearest businesses to your proposed location complementary to yours, or do they compete with you? (For example, a bridal-wear shop would be complementary to a Luv's Brownies® shop, because its customers would also be interested in my products. A competing bakery could only be bad for my business.)
- What kind of lease will be involved? How long of a commitment will it be? How easy or hard would it be to change the terms?

Part 4: Your Competition

This is a crucial section. As you are moving ahead, you must keep an eye out for the competition. Grab their marketing information, check out their websites, or call them and ask questions as if you were a customer. Make sure you know exactly what is going on around you, as this is the heart of your company's strategy for competitive advantage. Completing this exercise will give you a good start toward creating a unique selling proposition, which will be discussed later.

- Where is your competition located?
- How many competitors do you have?
- What makes you different?
- How do you expect to take sales away from your competitors?

Part 5: Your Distribution

How will you reach your intended audience—retail or other channels? (In my business, that would be groceries, delis, and similar businesses on the retail side, and the Internet and bridal fairs as alternative channels.)

- Do you plan to use sales reps?
- Will your business offer mail-order sales? Online orders via the Internet?
- How will new customers find out about your business?
- Will you use direct mail? E-mail? Personal contacts? Purchased leads?
- Will you advertise, and if so, how? Magazines and newspapers? Online web banners? Television? Window signs? Flyers?
- Can you think of an interesting "hook" for a feature story about your business in print or broadcast media?
- Do you plan to sell at trade shows?
- List any other marketing ideas you may have.

Part 6: Your Sales

- What are your costs for your merchandise and materials?
- How much money will you need for personal expenses?
- How much will you have to sell to break even?

- What are your total monthly and annual sales projections after one year of operation?
- What factors outside your control—such as the economy or changes in consumer behavior—could affect your projected sales?

Part 7: Your Key Personnel

- Who is in charge of day-to-day operations?
- How many employees will you have?
- Do you have consultants on your payroll?

Part 8: Your Organization

- What form of organization—sole proprietorship, corporation, S-corporation, or partnership—have you chosen?
- If you've chosen a corporation, who is on your corporation's board?
- If your business is a partnership, list your partners and their percentages of ownership.

Writing the Plan

Once you have finished your homework, you'll be ready to write your plan. A number of resources are available to help you. Any public library has many books dedicated to the subject. If you are using Quicken for your financial software, as I do, you might want to take a look at its Small Business Center (www. quicken.com/small_business/start/). The government's Small Business Administration offers a Small Business Planner website (www.sba.gov/smallbusinessplanner/index.html) that includes sample business plans and other helpful resources.

There are also a number of software applications that can help you write a plan. As you would with any computer program, ask around or search the Internet to find reviews of the various packages from actual users.

As you might expect, there are also professional business-planning consultants that you can hire to write your plan for you—but doing so will probably cost you thousands of dollars. For many small businesses, it may be smarter to pay an accountant for a few hours of help and write it yourself.

There are a number of different kinds of business plans, but they all fall into one of two primary categories: internal plans for you and any comanagers you have, and plans for external audiences, such as potential investors or loan sources.

Internal Plans

- *The feasibility study.* Here you crunch the numbers to determine whether it makes sense to start the business at all. Can you cover its losses until it becomes profitable, and is it ever likely to become profitable enough to recoup those losses, grow, and thrive?
- *The operational plan.* This is what I rely on—the emphasis is on what to do now and over the next few years, with finite goals and deadlines to keep you on course.
- *The expansion plan.* Let's say that you already have a business but are planning to launch a new product line or service, or that you're merging with another business. All of your financial calculations and your marketing and advertising plans must be completely revised. If the proposed changes are truly radical, do a feasibility study first.

Plans for External Audiences

Plans written for potential investors are usually *start-up plans*, as investors generally want to invest in a business at the very beginning. The form and spin of an external presentation will depend on the kind of investor you are dealing with.

- *Angels.* This business term comes from the theater world. Angels are amateur investors who may have a personal interest in you or the business; the classic angels are an entrepreneur's parents. Angels are often the least-demanding investors when it comes to proof of profitability, but by the same token, you should be particularly concerned about setting limits on what they might lose if the business is unsuccessful.

- *Venture capitalists.* These are highly desirable investors to have, though most small businesses are not likely to interest them. Venture capitalists have anywhere from tens of thousands to millions of dollars to invest. They are not afraid of high risk, but that is only because they expect the risk to be offset by the chance of extremely high profits. You will have to prove that a sizable market exists and that you are uniquely qualified to tap it in a big way.

- *Banks.* The loan department of a bank, on the other hand, doesn't want to hear anything about high risk. Their only concern, reasonably enough, is that you can demonstrate a high likelihood of repaying the loan on time. Dot every "i" and cross every "t" on the financial data you submit.

- *Government agencies, such as the Small Business Administration.* If you happen to qualify for a government loan, the agency you deal with is likely to be somewhat less anxious about repayment than a bank. But your approach should be similar, and the lender will still want every assurance that you know what you're doing.

A General Outline

I won't suggest a specific outline or template for you to follow in writing up your plan, as the details will depend heavily on the nature of your product or service and the audience you are addressing. But here are the basics that are likely to appear, in one form or another:

- *The executive summary.* This section is only necessary for plans designed for external audiences, but it is probably the most important section of the document to those readers. The executive summary should be positioned first—even before the table of contents—because many investors don't really read anything else. It is a pitch that briefly hits all the highlights of the plan in one upbeat narrative. Some books or websites will advise you to write the executive summary first, claiming that when you find a spin and approach that gets you excited, you can shape the rest of the plan to fit it. I completely disagree. In my opinion, it is more sensible and honest to write the summary last; that way, it will reflect the facts and not wishful thinking or persuasive hype.

- *Company history and management background.* These two sections are also for external audiences only. If your company or your management team has already notched major accomplishments, you'll want potential investors to know about them.
- *Products and services.* In this section, describe what you're selling in detail, including prospective offers that aren't quite ready yet. Compare your products and services with those of your competition. What advantageous differences can be exploited?
- *Operations summary.* Here you can describe your locations and any departments or divisions you have; what it costs you to operate your business in terms of supplies, labor, transportation, and so forth; and the day-to-day logistics of the business in action.
- *Market analysis.* Describe the total likely market for your product or service, how much of it you are reaching now, and how much you are likely to reach in the future.
- *Marketing and advertising strategy.* Describe your integrated marketing plan—not just advertising, but pricing and distribution as well. A good way to list prospective marketing and advertising programs is in ascending order by cost, positioning the least expensive ideas first. After all, that's almost certainly the order in which you will

implement them, so that's the order in which you will see results over time. Depending on the nature of your business, your website might merit a section of its own.

- *Strategic partnerships.* If you are working with another company, such as a channel partner, describe the relationship here. Discuss its costs and benefits, and where you expect the relationship to go in the future.
- *Financial plan.* Here's where you make your sales and profit predictions, backed up with real numbers: profit-and-loss statements, balance sheets, and projections for cash flow and return on investment. Include numeric goals and timetables.
- *Exit strategy.* You're less likely to need this section for an internal plan, but venture capitalists will always want to see it. Describe a plausible way for the investor to cash out in five or ten years—probably as the result of a merger, acquisition, or public stock offering. You don't need to worry about this section if your small business is your dream job, and you're in it for life.

Pitfalls to Avoid

1. Don't be unrealistic about capital, cash flow, or profits. Too many newcomers to small business entertain an "If I build it, they will come" fantasy. Their business plans project profits from the very first month, as they imagine their projected customer base will find them right away. *This never happens.* Look at the big boys, like Amazon.com. Large companies fully expect to run in the red for *years* before becoming profitable, so they line up massive resources in advance. They are able to get the investors they need only because they have a persuasively realistic plan. They can't fool themselves, and neither should you. It will take time for you to build a customer base, and you will have to support yourself for as long as it takes. This is why I recommend starting small and keeping your day job.

2. Don't skimp on the numbers. Your plan should set goals and timetables with hard dollar figures attached. It's the only way you can be sure, six months or a year from now, that you are moving toward profitability and not just bleeding money. If you feel you are guessing in the dark about what those numbers are going to be, then you are not in a position to go forward. You need to work with an accountant, or someone already familiar with this particular business and its market, until you have numeric goals that are realistic and meaningful.

Build on Your Plan

Once you have a sound initial plan, use it as a foundation on which to build. Once I had the business of catering brownies well in hand, I was able to explore new avenues.

I ventured out to trade shows and bridal fairs. I developed channel partners such as grocery stores, which bought my gift baskets at wholesale prices and retailed them under my Luv's Brownies® label and packaged my brownies under their own labels.

I offered a line of sugar-free brownies for people with diabetes and partnered with the American Diabetes Association and a local diabetes association for activities and events.

Because I knew that mortgage companies and banks are always looking for gift items for their best customers, I made a few phone calls to friends of friends and asked if they would put me on their catering lists. The very next day, I received a $500 order.

At events such as art and wine festivals, most people don't think twice about a $1 expenditure. My promotional Luv Bites® (bite-sized, heart-shaped brownies) sold for only a dollar each, but they filled the air with the smell of fresh-baked brownies and pulled the crowd in my direction. Once, the smell of the Luv Bites® enabled me to sell $2,000 worth of bottled water!

I don't make much money when children sell my products for high school fund-raisers, but that's okay. Those little feet on the street are like a free advertising force for Luv's Brownies®.

During key holiday periods (Valentine's Day, Mother's Day, and Father's Day), I often rent kiosks at shopping centers to sell brownie gift baskets, balloons, roses, and—of course!—bottled water. And guess what? In that venue, the bottled water was the $1 bargain that made people stop, see, and buy the rest of my offerings.

You never have just one business. Unless it's . . .

Your Business Is You

What it all comes down to is this: your business is *you*—your ideas and energy, your talents and abilities, your processes for making or selling products. Remember this when the time comes to market and promote your business.

Everyone you know, every passion you have, and everything you've ever done—all of these things are potential resources you can use to put your business across to the public.

You Are the Center of a Network

I realized that I needed a website immediately after starting Luv's Brownies®. I could have created my own. Certainly, there are many inexpensive software packages out there that will help you do it, and many web-hosting companies supply customers with free site-building applications. But you get what you pay for. The site you create as an amateur is likely to look like exactly that—an amateur site.

You might be surprised to find that the moment you start talking to your friends about putting a shop up on the Internet, some will reveal that they're already there. Usually, they'll be happy to share their experiences and may even point you to another friend who knows even more. That friend just might be able to help you create a semi-professional site for the price of a dinner or a little bartering of your product.

Internet storefronts were still pretty primitive in 1996. The friend who designed my first site had to build every Web page and price list individually. In the end, the site had more than 3,000 static and nonconnected pages. After about five years of that, I moved over to Yahoo! Shopping, a turnkey solution for small businesses. At Yahoo! Shopping, I only had to fill in templates with content and pictures, and the pages were automatically generated.

When it comes to the Internet, we are living in a pioneer age. Just as pioneers used to raise barns for each other, friends and coworkers will often be happy to help you build your website or to share their knowledge of the challenges of doing business on the Internet.

Your Charities Are Opportunities

As you search for venues to promote your business, consider charities and other community groups. They are always sponsoring sales and promotions of various kinds. There are many advantages to partnering with fund-raisers.

- *You are doing good things for your community.* If you pay for a stall at a trade show, pass out literature, and fail to get a nibble from a single customer, it's a total loss. But going home from an event knowing that you supported a worthwhile community project is something no one can take away from you.
- *There are more tangible benefits for you.* You probably won't have to pay for the space where you set up. The charity will pay to advertise the event and bring people past your stand. It's an inexpensive way to get exposure.
- *It's an excellent opportunity for networking.* The people you meet at an event of this kind tend to include community or church leaders and organizers of other types of events. And you're not just meeting them—you're meeting them in a context that makes the best possible personal impression.

Here are some examples of programs Luv's Brownies® has participated in:

- *Women's Expo.* This event, sponsored by KMEL, a San Francisco radio station, was a community-oriented promotion for woman-owned businesses in the Bay area. This is a great example of how the contacts you make cascade toward greater success. A KMEL DJ, Chuy Gomez, was so supportive of my business at the event that in six hours, I made about $2,000. After the event, I thanked Chuy for the free radio publicity, and he said, "Let's do something for Father's Day." I ran a Father's Day promotion on KMEL that offered Brownie Points (free delivery or FedEx shipping for any of Luv's Brownies® products) to all KMEL listeners. For a solid week, the name of my business was broadcast to thousands of listeners *free of charge*. KMEL benefited, too, because listeners like stations that provide giveaways. Even listeners who didn't win became curious about the Luv's Brownies® product and visited the website to request brochures. Later many of the brochure requests turned into orders for wedding favors, gift baskets, or brownie cakes.

- *The Barnes & Noble Women of Taste event.* This was a nonprofit sale held by Girls Inc., a nationwide youth organization that sponsors educational programs meant to inspire girls to grow up "strong, smart, and bold." I found out about the event because of my affiliation with the Big Sisters organization in Santa Clara, California. Participants exhibited free of charge. I served fresh brownies, handed out cards to local merchants and vendors, got a chance to meet and mingle with some of the top chefs in the Bay Area, and made contacts with organizers for other nonprofit events. Most importantly, I networked with representatives of many high-tech firms in the area; some of these contacts told me about company-sponsored events that brought vendors on-site for Christmas or Valentine's Day to sell their products to company employees.

- *The American Diabetes Walk.* I attend this event every year and have handed out almost 1,500 samples to people participating in the walk. I have also donated many sugar-free brownies to the organization's summer day camp for children, and this usually generates some orders for children's parties. This venue allows me to reach a large audience without the expense of a newspaper or radio ad.

- *The Chocolate Festival.* This annual event benefits various organizations, including the San Mateo Emergency Winter Shelter and the Bay Area AIDS ministry. (I have a special interest in AIDS programs, of course.) Visitors pay $15 each to eat as much chocolate as they want. Mama Kake and I passed out samples of our wares at a free exhibition stand. In addition to being another excellent opportunity to promote products and hand out business cards, it offered the additional benefit of heavy advertising in the *San Francisco Examiner*'s Peninsula section.

Those examples should give you some idea of the range of opportunities available. Don't worry that your product or service doesn't have the perfect "hook" for a particular event. Let the organizers of the event decide that—they will probably be much more welcoming and inclusive than you might expect.

Look for opportunities to get your face in print or on TV, as long as the name of your business appears nearby. The best thing about print is that it lives. People hang on to their favorite magazines and newspapers. If you think you aren't photogenic, or that you aren't good at talking to crowds, perhaps someone else in your family can be the public face of your business, or maybe one of your employees would jump at the chance.

Don't assume that your little business isn't important enough to merit any television time. TV shows—particularly *local* TV shows—have to find material to broadcast 24 hours a day, 365 days a year. Sometimes they are desperate to fill time.

Think you're not a local news story? Think again. Just about anything that happens to one of your neighbors is more interesting to you than what happens to a vice president of Chile. That's human nature, and it's the first principle of local news. Well, guess what? You're local.

A good story is based on real content and human interest. People love hearing about how other people got started toward success. And what you're trying to do—start your own small business and make it a success—is one of the most popular daydreams in America.

As you can see, you've already got half a good local feature story, no matter who you are. The other half of the story will come straight from the individual facts of your life.

What made you so fed up with your old job that you decided you had to work for yourself? What disadvantages have you overcome? What problems have you solved? What funny, scary, or completely unexpected things happened to you in the first few months of running your business?

Never forget that your business is *you*. If your family has been running the same business for more than a hundred years, that's a story. In fact, that's the story of the Guittard family. They've been manufacturing chocolates in San Francisco since 1868, and I use their product in my brownies. Guittard's adventures during the Gold Rush and the San Francisco earthquake of 1906 still make great advertising copy.

If, like my mentor Mama Kake, you have baked and decorated gigantic cakes in the shape of public buildings, shopping centers, and even a 2,000-pound representation of a clown, that's a story. Your life—whatever it is—is always a little bit different from anyone else's, and that's what makes it interesting to other people.

Imagine sitting across the table from some great friends you haven't seen for a few years. What would you tell them about the first year of your business? Whatever story surprises them or gets them excited or makes them laugh is the story to tell a larger audience.

Maybe I've convinced you that you have a story. Now, how do you get it out there to advertise your business? Here's a thought: the next time you attend a public event, look for the local reporters covering it. If you're at a charity or community service event, it's guaranteed that there will be some sort of media presence. Seek the reporters out and cultivate them. Try your story out, and find out the names of their feature editors (if they're with newspapers) or feature producers (if they're with TV or radio stations).

Once you have names, pick a good season to pitch your story. Because of the nature of my business, Valentine's Day is a good hook for me. But there's always something. Maybe your city has just decided to renovate the area where your shop is located. Maybe there's an annual festival highlighting the kind of product you make. Maybe a movie is filming in your town, and you supplied your product to the makers, or a character in the movie is in a business similar to yours. Cast your net wide enough, be creative enough, and you can find a hook into some current event. (In the 2006 Christmas season, a Chicago-area hot-dog stand got a tremendous amount of national press coverage by offering reindeer hot dogs.)

Then make your pitch. It's the same principle as a resume, only simpler. It should be no more than one short page. For your pitch to have the best chance, an editor or producer should be able to read it in 30 seconds. Use bullet points rather than complete sentences. The lead-in sentence can be as simple as "After meeting and talking with your reporter X, and hearing that event Y is coming up, I thought you might be interested in the feature possibilities of my business Z." Then hit them with everything interesting about you and your business as bullet points, and finish with contact information. It's that simple.

Don't waste your time or theirs with a hard sell, and don't try to write the story—that's their job. Just send in the information. If they need to fill time or space, *they* will contact you and *they* will build the story. I have been featured in many magazines, and no two stories have been alike. If the editors are booked up, they'll file your letter and perhaps call you the same time next year. But it costs you nothing to try, and if you do get a free media spread out of it, that's publicity that would cost you thousands to buy. Best of all, it will have far more credibility with the audience because you didn't buy it. It's news.

When pitching my story to the press, I've always allowed them to develop the angle. I just presented the facts and allowed the press to do their thing. But I have been in more than 40 printed publications to date, including:

- *Atlanta Voice*
- *Black Enterprise*
- *Ebony*
- *Essence*
- *Every Day with Rachael Ray* (Luv's Brownies® featured as one of Rachael's Faves)
- *New York Beacon*
- *Oakland Tribune*
- *Pastry Art & Design*
- *Rolling Out Magazine*
- *San Jose Magazine*
- *San Jose Mercury Newspaper*
- *Sun/Cupertino Courier*
- *Tennessee Tribune*
- *Today's Black Woman*
- *Upscale Magazine*

My story has also been covered on local and national television, including the Montel Williams show. Newspapers, magazines, and radio and television stations are all looking for stories all the time, and your story may be better than mine.

Stop right here. Put down this book for a while and think about *your* story. Tell it to yourself from the beginning. "This is how I started my business." Tell yourself where you want to go with it, what market you will be satisfying five years from now, and what sidelines you dream of moving your business into. Notice how spinning the story out for an imaginary listener changes your view of what the business is, why its product matters to you, and why it should matter to your customers. Don't stop spinning your yarn until you have a strong sense of how the company and its destiny are completely interwoven with your personal life.

Later chapters will build and elaborate on this idea. As you promote, market, and advertise your business, you'll be putting yourself out there. Get your story straight now.

Me with Montel Williams. I was featured on his show in 1999.

Design and Document Repeatable Processes

One of the most important ideas I hope to communicate is the importance of implementing repeatable processes in your business.

First of all, a *process* is any task that involves following a checklist of smaller tasks. Picking up the phone when it rings is not a process; it's a simple action that you don't have to think about. But answering the phone and taking a customer's order actually involves following a list of actions. An example of an order-taking process might be:

- Answer the phone within a few rings, before the customer hangs up.
- Identify yourself clearly and politely.
- Determine what the customer wants to order.
- Obtain payment information and shipping information.
- Make a useful, permanent record of the information.
- Set the customer's expectations for delivery.
- Transmit or process the payment and delivery information.

Depending on the nature of your business, the order-taking process might be a lot more complicated than that, or it might be that simple—but the point is, if you don't follow everything on your own list that constitutes your ordering process, you will run into problems. Remember, your order-taking process may seem simple to you, but it might not be so simple to everyone. Try this mental experiment:

Imagine your own little home business is doing so well that customer orders are coming in all day. If you're busy taking orders all day, you won't be able to fill them all. Therefore, you decide to hire someone to take the orders for you. I doubt you'd simply say to your new employee, "Take orders from customers," and let her work a process out for herself by trial and error. Instead, you'd carefully teach her your process and drill her on the complete list of tasks she must do. In fact, you'd probably teach her the process and then hand her a written checklist of the process's tasks so she could be sure of getting it right the first time, and every time.

That's why it's called a *repeatable* process. Once you have figured out what all the necessary steps are and written them down, a total stranger with minimal training can walk in and repeat the process perfectly just by going down the list.

A Simple Way to Deal with Complex Problems

I first encountered the process model while working in customer service at Hewlett Packard. HP customers who reached me might be looking to:

a) ask questions about products,
b) order something, or
c) get technical assistance for a product that's already been purchased

Every one of these choices can break down into additional sub-choices. In case c, for instance, the customer may need to speak with a hardware or software engineer, go to a Web page to read instructions, discuss buying an add-on service, or many other possibilities. Perhaps the customer did not purchase a service contract, and thus he would have to pay for the technical support. A customer service representative must be as ready as possible to address any customer need. In order to do this, representatives need to have access to documentation on a wide variety of specific processes, or checklists of tasks, that may involve 20 or 30 action items. When I worked at HP, every customer service rep had a constantly updated master binder of processes or procedures that was as large as a phone book.

No one—not even the brightest or most experienced member of the department—could possibly know every detail of all the different processes. But because all of the possibilities had been carefully thought through, divided into the necessary subtasks, and written down, anyone who could read—even a temp with just a few days' training—could successfully repeat a process by simply looking it up and following the checklist.

That is the power of a repeatable process. It simplifies training of staff and can facilitate automation.

Repeatable Processes Create Reliability

Ray Kroc, the genius behind the expansion of the McDonald's fast-food empire, is a classic example of a man who created and sold a process that was far more important than the hardware it used. A milkshake-machine salesman, he was impressed by the fast-food-by-the-numbers process devised by Dick and Mac McDonald and convinced them to allow him to take over the franchising end of the business.

The most important thing about the idea was that it truly was a turnkey solution. Once the McDonald brothers and Kroc realized the potential of creating food in a fast repeatable process, they realized they could sell the food cheaply and create a truly unique restaurant. Today, McDonald's has restaurants in 120 countries worldwide.

Other chains have piggybacked their way to success by grasping the same repeatable process concept. Today, Subway, which was founded in 1965, has more than 26,500 restaurants in 86 countries and is the world's largest submarine sandwich chain. The secret behind the company's rapid expansion is simple—Subway devised a process that lets a very small staff create a wide range of sandwiches that a customer can feel confident will be of consistent quality every time.

Individual workers have individual flaws. Even their virtues can get in the way sometimes—for example, creative people often have problems with consistent performance, which they may regard as dull. But a well-written process always delivers the same desired outcome, every time.

Repeatable Processes: Benefit from Experience

After doing extensive research on the McDonald's and Subway models, I decided to create my own repeatable process. After all, the key to my success in business has always been conducting careful research on other businesses and documenting their best practices.

First, I researched successful bakeries, and then I researched unsuccessful ones and tried to see the defining differences between the two. I found that the most successful bakeries had well-defined processes they have followed religiously.

I also found that talking and working side by side with an experienced professional in your industry will allow you get the inside scoop on how you should run your business. I would often do trades with my mentor, Mama Kake. Mama Kake would ask me to decorate or deliver cakes, answer phones, purchase products, or greet customers, and she would allow me to bake my brownies with her equipment, free of charge. If you are flexible enough, you will find that this sort of barter arrangement is not hard to arrange for any small business.

Just to get my feet wet, I frequently spent volunteer time at Mama Kake's. I needed to know everything about how a bakery worked and to thoroughly understand its daily challenges. I also talked to Mama Kake's accountant to uncover the financial dos and don'ts of the bakery business. I was happy to hear that the bakery I chose to learn from had been in business for over 30 years. This told me that the owner's repeatable processes were robust and time-tested. I confidently proceeded to study them and adapt them to my own business.

Me with my mentor, Mama Kake (Kathy McDonald), of Kathy's Kakes in San Mateo, CA.

Repeatable Processes Can and Should Include the Customer

Mama Kake taught me about the value of understanding your customer's needs. That might sound obvious to you. Don't most companies claim that in their organizations, the customer is always right, and that they always put customers first? In reality, however, even the smartest corporations are easily seduced into putting their own needs over those of their customers—and then end up paying for the mistake.

In 2003, Dell Computers made headlines when it decided to return some of its customer support lines from India, where they had been outsourced, back to the United States. Dell had chosen to outsource to India because of the significant cost savings, but mounting customer complaints about the quality of support and clarity of the customer service representatives drove the company to reevaluate its business decision.

You must always remember that the smaller your business is, the more directly you will interface with your customers; thus, you must do whatever you can to meet their needs.

Mama Kake once told me she redesigned her customer order form several times before she was satisfied with it. Mama Kake's bakery offers more than 200 custom made-to-order cake options, and the order form had to make the customer aware of every available option. At Luv's Brownies®, I decided to mirror Mama Kake's process for ordering, because it enabled customers to know all the available options and set their expectations of what they will receive, and when they will receive it. For example, Luv's Brownies® heart-shaped brownie cakes have to be hand-delivered because of their delicate butter cream frosting; therefore, they are only available in the San Francisco Bay Area. The mail-order gifts, such as the unfrosted brownies and Luv Bites®, can be shipped nationwide via FedEx. This is a significant issue that customers should be aware of before making a selection.

When setting up your own ordering process, I strongly suggest that you let your website work for you. Have your website forms collect as much information from the customer as possible. This makes the process at the back end easier for you to manage, and makes it easier for you to allocate your resources and your time. This also benefits the customer: She reviews the clear-cut questions and answers them at her own pace, she can make corrections as needed, and she's assured that issues like spelling errors won't compromise the order (unless she makes them!). Remember that these website forms are a process as well, and think long and hard about whether you've included all the necessary steps and choices.

Whenever you are crafting a process that interacts directly with a customer, it is a good idea to review it from the customer's perspective. Role-play it. Pretend that you are the customer. What do you want and need to hear? What questions might you want to ask? Also—what mistaken ideas might you have about the business and the product, as an outsider? Run through this role-playing process with your paper order forms, your website order forms, and your phone-order protocol.

Next, slip into the role of the person who will take a phone order. Does the phone-order process that you've documented answer customer questions? Does your process explain things to the customer that he might have mistaken ideas about?

A good customer service process must work smoothly from both directions. The person who answers your business phone may not know everything about your business, and you can be sure that the customer who's calling doesn't. Remember that your documented order-taking process is designed to meet the needs of both of these participants, and that it isn't complete until both parties get everything they need from it.

Once you have a bulletproof process, it can be adapted to different circumstances. For instance, Luv's Brownies® customers can place orders in five different ways:

- By phone: (408) 881-0759
- By using the website: www.luvsbrownies.com
- By fax: (408) 246-8594
- By mailing the online order form or brochure insert to: 2910 Stevens Creek Blvd. #109 San Jose, CA 95128
- By personal contact: A customer at a bridal fair, where I

sell directly, or a channel customer, like a grocery store, florist, or limo service, can place a pen-and-paper order.

By imagining these various scenarios from the perspective of both a first-time customer and a first-time employee, I was able to create a single order form that captured all of the necessary information. I use the same form in all five order-taking venues.

Repeatable Processes: Getting the Most from Temporary Workers

Employees are very expensive. Once I realized that employees were my second highest expense, I knew that temporary employees were the best option for Luv's Brownies®.

I have always hired temps, who are paid by the hour or by the job, on a project-by-project basis. During peak times, such as Valentine's Day, Mother's Day, or Christmas, I hire additional temporary workers to bake, deliver, handle administrative duties, return phone calls, and follow up on customers' requests. Some bakeries streamline their position plans, and employees are trained for only one or two different responsibilities. Instead, I insist that my employees are cross-trained in all departments, so if one person calls in sick, someone else can cover for her.

I've often asked sales associate in stores for assistance and gotten the response, "That's not my department." An employee should always be able to assist you—if only by getting you to the right person. I have built a team-driven environment where any employee can play any position. How do I get so much from my people? By giving them clear-cut and repeatable processes to follow.

I often use staff from Kelly Temporary Employee Services and have had nothing but good experiences with them. My Kelly staffing coordinator has always sent me high-quality workers. Their hourly rates are very expensive, however, so I must make sure that every new temp can hit the ground running after reviewing the clearly articulated documentation I've prepared for his responsibilities.

For example, I once wrote a position plan for a trade show coordinator. The temp prepared herself by reviewing the website and learning about all of Luv's Brownies® bakery products. A few days before the show, I would ask her random questions about the products Luv's Brownies® offered, just to see if she was up to speed. If I thought that she was well-informed about all the products, she would be allowed to work at the trade show. She would then be responsible for greeting potential customers, handing out literature, serving fresh brownies, taking orders, and answering questions.

This was a case where the processes definitely had to include the customer. I made sure that my Trade Show Coordinator Kit included a list of frequently asked questions. I generated the necessary questions by playing different roles in my head: the temp, the curious consumer, and potential channel partners like bakeries, limousine services, and florists. This manual included a list of suppliers, a pricing guide, a copy of my business license, health-code and food regulations for trade shows, a contact list, and even a list of ingredients for the regular and sugar-free baked goods, which is often requested by customers with diabetes.

Once the kit was complete, I was confident that a temp could handle anything that came up. There was another nice dividend, as well: Because I'd put together a list of questions that covered everything for everyone, it wasn't hard to boil down a subset that could be printed up and handed out as point-of-purchase materials for customers.

There's no end to the benefits of a good process checklist.

Developing Your Own Repeatable Processes

Perhaps your dreams of running your own business have nothing to do with baking. The power of repeatable processes applies to any business.

The time to start developing repeatable processes is at the very first phase of your enterprise—when you are probably the only employee, and you're using your own common sense to solve every problem as it comes up.

- *Think ahead.* Imagine this: you just figured out the best way to keep track of receipts and order resources so you always have enough for this week's production. Don't wait another second—write that process down! Do it now, while you remember all the steps and the best order in which to do them. Even if you're absolutely sure you'll remember the process the next time it comes up, remember that you are also documenting it for your employees.

- *Don't worry about getting your process description right the first time—you probably won't.* As you gain more experience in your business, you'll begin to notice the wide variety of special cases you will encounter, and you'll realize that your process will need many more steps to cover every possibility. Don't let that discourage you. If you start early, while your process is simple, the process will just need to be tweaked later. If you faithfully update your process as you learn more from your business, every worker in your business will be able to profit from your experience.

- *Include input from your employees.* If you have employees, they're getting plenty of experience too, and they may be encountering situations that you may not have documented. That's great! Have them review the documentation you've prepared and encourage them to add anything that may have been missed.

Processes should be created to follow the flow of how people naturally work. In my experience, that means they have to be developed from the bottom up. When people who are actually doing the job create processes, the input is coming from a reliable source. When management is dictating the process flow, the folks at the bottom of the food chain tend to generate a lot of questions, concerns, and confusion. I have had to work with processes written from both directions, and I know what I'm talking about.

Thus, one of the most important processes your new business will have is a process for writing, amending, and storing processes. Never make the mistake of thinking that documentation is a waste of time. Developing repeatable processes saves time, money, and trouble, and it's never too early, or too late, to start.

Design an Integrated Marketing Campaign

Why You'd Rather Be First than Best

While I was pursuing my MBA, one of my professors, Dr. David Palmer, told me to start my business. He said, "If you don't do it, someone else will, and you will always wonder what you could have done with your passion." I took a leave of absence from school and headed into entrepreneurship. (I eventually finished the MBA program in December 2004.)

In addition to illustrating the importance of developing a business and marketing plan, Dr. Palmer taught me urgency. In the competition for the consumer's mind, he would say, it is more important to be the first to deliver a product or service category than to be the best. The concept of "brand management" is an excellent illustration of this idea.

All of us have used the terms Kleenex to mean tissues, Xerox to mean a photocopier, and Scotch tape to mean cellophane tape. These products were the first of their kind to register on the national brand consciousness. They may be the best of their kind, or they may not be, but they are still the first names that come to mind when many of us consider making a purchase in these categories. And that's half the ball game.

Being first means you can actually define the look and feel of the product. For example, if you are the first to invent a key software application, like the spreadsheet, your competitors will discover that they can't sell their version unless its files are compatible with your system, because that is the first feature that every customer asks for. And every customer asking for it will probably ask himself, "Hmm. Why don't I just go with the original?"

And your advantage doesn't just extend to new buyers. As long as your product or service delivers satisfactory results, the early adopters who chose you will be highly reluctant to change to a competitor. This is partly common sense on their part, but psychological factors also operate in your favor. The first customers for a new idea feel like pioneers and winners too, and they will associate that feeling with your company. First love is often the strongest. Consider how people feel about their iPods!

When you drive a stake in the ground and make your brand the first in its category, your competitors can't do anything else but get in line behind you. Like a pioneer in a new land, you have first knowledge of its resources. For a business, that means you will be the first to discover markets, suppliers, and potential partners.

Three Ways to Maintain First Place

An additional perceived value of having been first is uniqueness. As competitors copy every possible aspect of your product or service, how can you maintain this uniqueness? There are at least three tools at your disposal:

- Trademarks
- Patents
- Trade secrets

Trademarks. What is a trademark? It is a name, symbol, logo, slogan, or design feature that is distinctive and used to identify your business and its products to consumers. (A service mark is the same concept in the world of services.) The Metro-Goldwyn-Mayer lion is a trademark, the golden arches in front of every McDonald's is a trademark, and the phrase "Home of the Original Heart-Shaped Brownie®" is a trademark. As you see, the concept takes many forms. When you create a trademark and establish it by using it in the marketplace, you are asserting that it is your property and that it cannot be used by others.

The flip side of that idea is that you cannot claim ownership of a trademark that is already in use by another company or that is already in common use in the public domain. For example, if your last name happens to be Dole and your business is selling apples by the side of the road, you can't claim the trademark "Dole Apples," because it's already taken; you can't claim the trademark "Apples," because that's the English-language word for the product that is already in common use by everyone; and you can't claim "Red Apples" or "Sweet Apples," because those adjectives are already commonly associated with the concept of apples. But Apple Computers and Apple Music are valid trademarks because no one associated the word Apple with either computers or music until those companies established the mark.

Some of the rules for what you can trademark and what you can't are highly technical. The best place to research your intended trademark is the website of the U.S. Patent and Trademark Organization (USPTO) (http://www.uspto.gov/main/trademarks.htm).

You don't have to register a trademark; you can merely assert your rights by putting the letters "TM" at one corner of your logo or slogan, but there are legal and practical benefits of registering your trademark with the government. While you're doing your research on the USPTO website, you can search the public database of registered trademarks to make sure that you are not infringing on a trademark already in use. The consequences of doing so can be expensive and embarrassing.

Back in 1976, the National Broadcasting Corporation (NBC) decided to trademark a new logo for use in literature, signage, and other advertising all over the world. Thousands of assets had to be reprinted or repainted, which made for a very expensive makeover. Almost immediately after launching its new logo (an N in the shape of two yoked trapezoids), NBC discovered that it was identical except for its color to that of the Nebraska ETV Network, a chain of PBS affiliates. Clearly, Nebraska ETV was in the same business as NBC, and public confusion could result from the simultaneous use of both logos. It was accidental but still trademark infringement, and rather than go to the expense of remaking all its logo-bearing possessions again, NBC had to settle with Nebraska ETV and pay for *its* new logo and all related expenses.

The moral of this story? Before investing heavily in a trademark, make sure that it is distinctive and that no one in the same business is doing anything similar.

When you first start a small business, you may not have any trademark to speak of. Your signage will probably be generic, and your logo may be as simple as the first letter of your name. But if you're the first in a new field, the sooner you get a distinctive identifying mark in front of the public, the better.

Once you have a recognized national trademark, you are not home free. You must defend the trademark against infringement. If you passively let other entities use it, it can eventually be considered common property, and you will lose your rights to it.

As I'd mentioned earlier, Kleenex has a tremendous advantage, because its distinctive name is so well-known that people think of or say the trademark whenever they visualize a facial tissue. (Who even uses the phrase "facial tissue?") By zealously enforcing its rights and reminding people that Kleenex is a registered trademark and proper name and not a word in the dictionary, the owners have kept their mark from being "genericized." As a result, no other company can sell Acme Kleenexes. At one time, aspirin was also a brand name, but the owner of its trademark allowed it to lapse into generic use, and now anyone making acetylsalicylic acid can use the name.

A distinctive and zealously enforced trademark can help you keep the advantage of being first with a product.

Patents. Patents and trademarks are often confused in casual speech, but they are very different. A trademark is an identifying sign or symbol for a company; it is meant to keep one company from passing off its wares as the product of another company, and it can stay in force indefinitely. A patent is an officially granted right to exclusively exploit a new invention for a certain period of time. The lucrative returns to the inventor that are possible during this time are meant to encourage invention and innovation. The patent also aids the technological and commercial development of society by officially publishing all the details of how an invention works, so after its expiration, others can try to perfect or further develop the idea. Because the patent exists, inventors have a strong profit incentive to develop useful new inventions; because the patent expires, the public will eventually get the product at a low price, and future inventors will be able to build on the idea and make new advances.

If a drug company spends millions of dollars developing a life-saving drug, a patent gives the company a monopoly for a period of time. During that time, the company can earn back all of its development costs and a healthy profit. After the patent expires, anyone can manufacture and sell the drug, as the formula and manufacturing process are on record at the patent office.

Items that can be patented range from the design of a piece of hardware to the description of a manufacturing process. Because the stakes are higher, the rules governing what is distinctive, original, and useful enough to be patented are much more complicated than the rules for trademarks. The USPTO is the best resource to learn more.

If you are first in a new market because you actually invented your product and nothing like it existed before, a patent will give you a period of time (usually 20 years) without competition. That should be enough time to establish yourself in the public mind as the original—and the best.

Trade secrets. Perhaps 20 years doesn't strike you as a long time. Would you prefer to keep your monopoly forever? Then don't patent your invention. Just keep its details secret. This is the cheapest and simplest protection of all, if you can manage it. Food manufacturers and restaurants often take this route—often because their recipes and processes may not be considered distinctive or useful enough to receive a government patent anyway. McDonald's "secret sauce," KFC's coating recipe, and the formula for Coca-Cola are all the same: none of these inventions have ever been patented, and none have ever been perfectly copied.

If you can keep a secret, you can keep a monopoly.

Suppose You Weren't First in the Marketplace

Cheer up. Most of us won't be. Most products and services are not patented. Brownies had been around for quite a while before I started my business. Benchmarking yourself against your competition can help you carve out your own advantage, and once you establish the value of what you offer, your trademark will acquire value.

If You Can't Be First, Be Different

You don't have to have a completely original idea to be brandable. Just make yourself different enough to avoid confusion.

My mentor, Mama Kake, really understands branding and the principle that "Your business is you." Even I usually end up calling her Mama Kake. She uses a color theme of chartreuse green and white for her bakery, and her staff (the Kupcakes) wears checkered aprons in those colors. She was the first bakery owner in our area to uniform her team. I was at a local eatery once where a San Francisco Giants game was silently playing on TV. Suddenly, someone in the restaurant said, "Kathy Kake, bake a gigantic cake for the Giants." I looked up at the screen and saw one of Kathy's uniformed employees in the stands. The patron had recognized Kathy and her Kupcakes from the chartreuse aprons alone.

Obviously, no one else is going to adopt the same bakery uniform—if they did, they would just give Mama Kake free advertising. But the basic idea of a consistent color theme that extends even to the aprons is a terrific branding idea that I could still make use of through *differentiation*.

My staff now wears red and white-checkered aprons during its deliveries. The color is different enough from chartreuse green, so there's no cross-brand confusion between Mama Kake and me. Since red is commonly associated with the heart shape, it ties the color scheme to the category in which I was first—the heart-shaped brownie. Believe me, it works! At bridal fairs, grocery stores, and coffee shops, everyone recognizes us. Nothing beats being your own walking advertisement.

Developing Your Unique Selling Proposition

The heart of your brand—your appeal to the customer—is your unique selling proposition, or USP. You should be able to boil it down to 10 words or less. But that doesn't mean that it's trivial. If you don't have a USP, you don't have a saleable product; if you don't have a saleable product, you don't have a business.

The Elements of a Unique Selling Proposition

The USP is a catchphrase or slogan that answers the three most important questions a customer has for you:

- *What are you trying to sell me?* You must make a clear-cut proposition.
- *Why should I want to buy it?* You must sell your product or service on the basis of value.
- *Why should I buy this from you in particular?* You must establish the *unique* quality of your product or your service.

All three elements have to be present in your USP. For instance, my USP is "Home of the Original Heart-Shaped Brownie®." Just six words beautifully answer all three questions:

- *What am I trying to sell you?* Brownies.
- *Why should you want to buy them?* They aren't just any brownies; their heart shape makes them an expression of love, like roses. Therefore, they're not just a treat that you might buy for yourself, but they're also suitable as a gift for your sweetie.
- *Why should you buy them from me in particular?* Even if

you could find them somewhere else, I've got the original version, and isn't the original always the best? And notice that word "home?" That suggests home cooking, indicating that my brownies have no preservatives, which further separates me from my competition.

The Key to All Three Questions

You must deliver real value to the customer, and you must add value that she can't easily find elsewhere. I'm going to discuss how to construct a winning USP in detail, but I want to stress this the most, because it is the single most important principle that underlies all three questions. If you get this part right, you can't go wrong. But without it, no clever words can make up the difference.

Suppose I had wanted to be in any business selling stuff in a shop, and thought, "Brownies. People like to eat 'em. I'll sell 'em and make money." I could have rented a shop and filled it with those plastic-wrapped brownies you see in vending machines or dime stores. I'd think, "I'm a great businesswoman! I can buy these mass-produced brownies dirt cheap, which means more profit for me when I sell them."

I would have gone broke in a week.

Why would anyone go to the trouble of finding my store and driving across town to get there just to buy not-very-good brownies they can get anywhere? Now, I'm not pretending the heart-shaped, home-baked brownie ranks with the invention of fire, but when you compare it with a vending-machine brownie, any customer can see the value I've added. That's what makes it a saleable product, and that's what gives me a business.

Bearing that principle in mind, let's look at the three elements of the USP again. What are the pitfalls in constructing a USP? How can you fall short?

Pitfall 1: The Proposition Is Unclear

Wait a minute, you might say. "The proposition is just 'What are you selling?'—right? There's no way to foul that up." Oh, but there is. In fact, there are two ways to foul it up—being too vague, and being too technical.

Vague. Consider this situation: I call up a friend, Annie, to ask about her new business.

"What's your proposition, Annie? What are you trying to sell me?"

"Well, I'm selling my services as a multi-tasking facilitator for functions."

"Annie, I love you, but I have no idea what you're talking about. What kind of 'functions'?"

"You know, parties, get-togethers, business meetings with refreshments."

"So you 'facilitate.' Are you a party planner?"

"No, I don't want to say party planner, because I do everything, I plan, I design and send out the cards, I cater, I tend bar—whatever you need."

"That's great, Annie, but you've got to say it like that, in English. Maybe your unique selling proposition should be 'All-purpose party help, from planning to tending bar.' Now I know what you're talking about, and I see how useful it would be. *That's* your proposition."

Use everyday language that says exactly what you mean. Avoid vagueness, and avoid the opposite problem: being too technical.

Next, imagine I'm talking to my genius friend Kai about the service he wants to sell.

"Kai, what's your proposition?"

"It's a simple matter of recalibrating the backwash manifold and bleed lines of your furnace to get the optimum advantage from new heat-exchange hardware I will install between the firewall and the—"

Two minutes later, he still isn't finished, but I cut in as he comes up for air.

"Kai, I know you've told me *exactly, precisely* what you're going to do, but I still don't know *why* you're doing it or what it will mean to me. If your description was an ad, I'd have turned the page a long time ago."

"I can't help it. It's a complicated process with a lot of steps. I'm selling you a piece of hardware for your furnace, but I'm also completely re-working your furnace so you get the benefits of it. Without all the adjustments, you don't get the full 33 percent fuel use reduction. See, it's not just the hardware, it's a whole system—"

"Sure, Kai, but you can simplify the whole proposition by summarizing the value you're offering: 'My system for cutting your fuel bills by one-third.' *That's* your proposition."

Be exact and concrete, but keep it simple. Express the basic idea in terms of how it serves the customer.

Pitfall 2: The Proposition Is Stated, But Not Sold

My friend Pilar's problem is that no one is joining her fitness center. "I don't know, Aundrea. There is a big gym across town, and maybe I just can't compete. They certainly have a lot of expensive weight machines that I don't offer."

"I see. But isn't there some value that you offer and they don't? Would you go to that big gym yourself?"

"Oh, no. For one thing, it's in bad part of town, and you have to park on the street. I'd be very uncomfortable walking alone there at night. In fact, the whole place isn't very female-friendly. It's mainly heavy irons for guys to pump—no Pilates equipment, like I have, and no areas set aside for stretching or yoga classes, which I offer. Did I tell you that?"

"No, and there's no way I could guess it from your storefront or your ads, either, Pilar. You just present yourself as a generic fitness center. Instead of hoping to get some of the business from a better-equipped gym, you have to emphasize everything you've got that it doesn't. A safe, relaxing atmosphere for women, Pilates, yoga—that's a lot of value, but unless it's on every sign and every ad, no one will discover it's there. Something like 'Pilar's Pilates Center, a safe place to stretch and grow stronger' would be a great proposition. That doesn't just say it, it *sells* it."

Pitfall 3: The Customer Is Sold on the Product, But Not on Your Unique Value as Supplier

There's no question that two elements of the USP—the selling points for the product and for you as the unique supplier—tend to blur together. When that happens, it's not necessarily a bad thing. If Kai's high-value furnace treatment is his own patented invention, no one else is offering it, so he has a unique proposition. By selling her fitness center on the value of its differences from the gym across town, Pilar is also branding herself as one of a kind—an alternative gym for women. But is Annie really the only party planner in town who also caters and tends bar? If this combination is actually pretty common, then she needs to add more value in order to stand out.

Don't make the easy mistake of relying on a purely cosmetic difference to make yourself unique. You can always come up with a memorable brand motif. Anything unusual is memorable. But does it add value?

Ed was a star quarterback for his high-school football team, the Alligators. He's now running a business called Alligator Used Cars. There's a big stuffed alligator in the lobby, the salesmen wear alligator boots, and the storefront and advertising materials boast a logo showing an animated alligator. Customers find the name to be very memorable and often pass it on to other people, so in that respect, it's good branding. But it's no help at all in establishing Ed's unique selling proposition, because alligators don't have anything to do with used cars, and the fact that every salesman wears alligator boots adds no value to the cars on the lot. A customer would have no particular reason to choose the Alligator team over any other used-car outfit; they're unique only in appearance, and not as suppliers of a unique value.

But there are all sorts of ways to supply a unique value. You don't have to be the inventor of the product or service, or the only person to combine one with another. Sometimes it's just a question of being in the right place at the right time.

Right Place, Right Time

"The Verger," a short story by Somerset Maugham, is about a middle-aged man who gets fired from his lifelong job as a church caretaker when it is discovered that he can neither read nor write. In the story, the man leaves his place of employment for the last time and walks the streets miserably, ashamed to go home to his family. He has some money saved, but what is he going to do now—an illiterate man with no experience in business?

He needs to come up with a plan before he gets home, so he decides to fill his pipe, thinking that a good smoke will help him clear his head and think. However, he's wandered into an unfamiliar part of town, and he can't find a smoke shop. He walks in wider and wider circles for hours and never finds a place that sells pipe tobacco. When he gets home, he's exhausted, and when his family hears his news, they assume that he feels terrible. But he doesn't. He now knows what to do with his savings—he has found the perfect location for a tobacconist's shop, which will be the only one in that part of town.

Sure enough, his shop is successful and the first in a chain of enterprises. He starts each one by scouting out neighborhoods on foot to see what the locals need and don't have.

Being the only product or service supplier of your kind in a particular area is a good way to offer unique value. But always remember that someone can take it away from you simply by moving in across the street.

When competition moves right into your neighborhood, you have to reset to zero and brainstorm every aspect of your business to see how it compares with your rivals. Like Pilar, you are looking for added value in the existing differences—but to create a USP, you may also have to deliberately create new differences.

It's worth considering another hypothetical case in greater detail, so you can get a feel for the sort of brainstorming that's involved.

"Here's my problem," says Nate. "I recently inherited a coffee shop from my aunt. It was a good business with a great in-town location on Fifth Street. It had a steady following until last year, when my aunt got sick and closed it up. I want to reopen, but now the Fifth Street Coffee Shack is surrounded—there's a Starbucks on Fourth Street and a Starbucks on Sixth Street. Is the situation hopeless?"

"Well, I wouldn't choose to start a new shop against competition like that," I tell him. "But as long as you've got the site and the equipment already, free and clear, it's worth trying to save the place. You've got your finger on the main point—it's all about the competition, and how you're going to beat them. Have you checked out the Starbucks shops?"

"Oh, yeah."

"What are they like?"

"Typical of the smaller Starbucks outlets, with nothing extra. They've got all the exotic flavors and sandwiches. They get the professional crowd from the financial district."

"And they've got all the advantages of repeatable processes," I add. "Any visitor from out of town can go there confident that they can get the same favorites they're used to, served the same way."

"You're not helping, Aundrea."

"I'm just being realistic, which is what you have to be. You can't fight them by being more of a Starbucks. You should make sure you're covering many of the same basics that are most popular there—lattes, espresso, and so on—but your unique selling proposition is going to have to be based on differentiation. The first way to brainstorm that is by direct attack: when you go into either Starbucks, what *don't* they have that you would *like* to have?"

Nate thinks it over. "If I'm alone, I always like to take my time over coffee and read. All Starbucks ever seems to have are old newspapers." He snaps his fingers. "You know, more and more bookstores are putting in coffee shops. Maybe my coffee shop should become a bookstore!"

"You might be replacing one tough business with another," I point out. "And putting in a good selection of new books would be a huge capital investment. But we don't give a flat 'No' to any idea in the brainstorming phase. Is there a way to add books without laying out much money?"

"Sure," Nate says. "If I visited yard sales and some consignment stores, I could probably fill two large bookcases with old bestsellers for $25 or less. I couldn't make much money selling them, but I could put up a sign, 'Take a book, leave a book.' A rotating library would be a pretty good attraction."

"And it would make the place a little more like home. What was your aunt's former clientele like?"

"Guys with delivery routes, cops, nurses and other staff members from a nearby hospital. Quite a few office workers on breaks. Yeah, they definitely liked the home-away-from-home touch."

"So let's build on that. Can they have pie with their coffee?"

"Sure, I could have a little display of snacks. But so does Starbucks, of course—very nice stuff from local upscale bakeries."

"But they don't bake it on site," I point out. "It's not home cooking. If you made your own coffeecakes and pies—"

"I couldn't match their selection."

"But you could beat their prices. And more importantly, anyone passing by on the street could *smell the goodies baking*."

A big smile grows across Nate's face. "You know, that's the best memory I have of a neighborhood coffee shop when I was a kid— that smell of pie baking. That's part of the reason I wanted to own a coffee shop in the first place."

"I see that all the time in my business," I say. "I won't work a trade fair anymore unless I can bake on site. Smell has the strongest emotional impact of any of the senses. Now, you and your competitors are equal in putting out the great smell of coffee, but if you add the aroma of rising dough and cinnamon, you're ahead of the game.

"You just mentioned something else—why you wanted to own a coffee shop in the first place. Brainstorm on that for a moment. What are the pictures that come into your head about an inviting place to drink coffee? Use your memories, think of old movies . . ."

"Okay," Nate says, closing his eyes. "We've already talked about the homey family place where neighborhood people can sit and gossip. I can build on that. I know they've got old photographs of Fifth Street from 50 years ago down at the library. I could get some copies blown up and hang them on the wall to play up the nostalgia angle. But you know, my other favorite image of a coffee shop is completely different. I think about a place I used to hang out when I was in college—a student place with alternative music, poetry magazines, concert flyers, and posters. Too bad I can't combine the two; there is a college nearby."

"Never say 'No' when you're brainstorming," I remind him. "The neighborhood folks and the college kids have one important thing in common—they aren't as willing to spend big bucks on a cup of coffee as the young professionals in the financial district are. The good news is that they also aren't so picky about having the latest and trendiest coffee from Nepal. Settle on a few good blends you can buy more cheaply in bulk—you can charge a little less and maintain your profit margin. And now you're not just talking about adding atmosphere—you're providing value.

"As far as putting those two different customer crowds together, maybe you can't, but maybe you don't have to. Suppose you broke your day in half. You'd get an older neighborhood trade in the morning and close up around two—"

"It gets pretty dead from two to five anyway," Nate admits.

"—and then reopen in the evening for the college crowd. Have open-microphone nights—that way, you're offering live music for free, or you can pay the performers in coffee. Perhaps you could do a poetry slam once a week, with a little gift-certificate prize. Some of the performers will bring in friends to see them.

"And it's easy to combine your two approaches in your name and slogan. 'The Corner Coffee Shop—Last of the Independents.'"

"That's great!" Nate says.

"Don't get too excited too soon. These are just experiments. Wait and see if they actually draw in customers before spending any real money on a makeover. But if everything works, you've got a unique selling proposition to base your advertising on, and that's the essential first step."

Putting It All Together

It's all about inspiration, research, brainstorming, and tweaking. I've already told you how the basic idea for Luv's Brownies came to me after praying for 24 hours straight, looking over at my childhood doll, Luv, and hearing myself say "heart-shaped brownies." I couldn't believe heart-shaped brownies hadn't been used as a brand before, and I only accepted that it was true after spending hours in the library doing searches about similar products. Then I built on my first inspiration, as you should when the time comes. As I told Nate, think back and recapture the emotional memories that underlie your idea and make it seem so special. In my case, it was the smell in the air while my dad was cooking Sunday dinners and the way that aroma made me feel completely at home. Home was the emotional key, and home cooking: "Home of the Original Heart-Shaped Brownie®."

When Atmosphere Won't Help

Of course, if you're selling hardware widgets and your competition is selling hardware widgets that do exactly the same thing, the smell of pies baking isn't going to help you.

Revisit the "Your Competition" part of your business and marketing plan. Write down your competitors' features and benefits and rank them against yours. It would be best for you to develop a spreadsheet of all your product offerings, services, and price points. Research, brainstorm, and tweak until you can come up with some bottom-line numbers that are better than the other guy's as well as your unique selling proposition, and hammer on them in your sample slogans. In a case like this, it's okay if the difference is small, as long as you're on the right side of it. "200 milliseconds faster for 10 cents less!" may not sound like much to the average person on the street, but the customer for your product does the same sort of research and comparisons. Once she knows what you're selling, what its added value is to her, and that you are the unique seller with that value, why would she pick the other guy?

In 1996, I was often asked, "What are Luv's Brownies?" Now that I've added the "Home of the Original Heart-Shaped Brownie®" to my website and all packaging, literature, and marketing, the only question I hear is, "Where can I buy them?"

Benchmarking Against Your Competition

This can make or break your company. It's important for you to know how your competition's product differs from yours in four key regards: quality, convenience of use, availability, and price. If you can't provide a significantly better value in at least one of these areas, you shouldn't be going head-to-head in that arena.

Convenience and Availability: Betamax versus VHS

In business magazines, you will often see the term "Betamaxed" used to describe a product that starts out as a market pioneer and leader—with all the advantages discussed in a previous chapter—only to be completely wiped out by its competition. This dates back to the duel between Sony's Betamax and the VHS videotape standard in the 1970s and 1980s.

Even though the result of this conflict is widely known, most people have a fuzzy or inaccurate memory of the details and sometimes derive the wrong lesson from it.

In the early days of recording video on tape, there were several different tape formats that were tied to different recorder technologies and were therefore incompatible. If you wanted to buy your own video recorder (and they were expensive at first—many people just rented them from the same place where they got the movie tapes), you had to make a hard decision between the only two formats that were likely to succeed: Betamax or VHS.

The way you often hear the story told is this: the Betamax was really the higher-value and higher-quality format, but VHS recorders were cheaper, and the backers of VHS were able to get more studios to release movies in their format; as a result, consumers had better rental choices in VHS. This created a downward spiral for Betamax, because as it became harder for buyers to find Betamax movies, more consumers defected to VHS, which made it less profitable for the studios to release movies for the shrinking Betamax customer base. That made Betamax movies even harder to find. Eventually Betamax lost the battle, even though—people will tell you—it was the "better" product. Just bad luck, people say.

There is no such thing as luck.

As business journalists like Jack Schofield and Geoffrey Moore have persuasively argued, this standard version of the story is at most half-true, and the moral is completely wrong. If a product is truly better at meeting the needs and desires of customers, it is very unlikely to fail in head-to-head competition. What is wrong with this story is its mistaken and incomplete notion of what "better" means.

Betamax was in fact the leader and pioneer in the video recording field, and VHS had to come from far behind to beat it. These are the true parts of the story: a) the picture quality of the Betamax tapes and tape players was superior to that of VHS because of higher horizontal resolution and lower video noise, although the difference was not as great as people would often lead you to believe; and b) Betamax was more expensive, but not as much more, and not for as long as is often said. This telling of the story also ignores the fact that Betamax was the pioneer: in the beginning, far *more* movies were available in Betamax format than in VHS.

So if Betamax had a small advantage in quality, and VHS had a small advantage in price—but most movies available to rent were in Betamax format—wasn't Betamax "better" overall? How did it lose its initially dominant market share?

You have to look at all four variables before you're looking at your product the way a consumer will. Betamax led in quality and availability, and lagged in price—but had completely ignored what turned out to be the deciding factor for consumers: convenience.

Again and again, I've been surprised to see that innovators in business don't realize the full potential of even their own inventions. Sony engineers refused to make a four-hour Betamax tape, because they believed the quality of such a tape would be too poor. They failed to see that the Betamax user might consider the power to record television to be at least as important as playing rental tapes. This was the fatal difference between the standards: while the VHS tape could record for a full four hours, the original Betamax cassettes had a capacity of only one or two hours at the most.

A Betamax owner couldn't set the machine for the starting time of a football game and then leave the house or go to bed; he'd have to quickly swap in a second cartridge in the middle of the recording time.

So Betamax was less convenient to use, in a way that also decreased its advantage. At first there were still more Betamax movies available for rent. But four-hour VHS tape cartridges enabled consumers to record multiple movies on a single tape, and it allowed sports fans to tape games without worrying about switching cartridges.

Thus, VHS had the advantage in price, convenience, and availability, and consumers shifted to the VHS format in a big way. Betamax fought back, developing a two-hour-plus tape and less expensive players, but all the efforts were too late to stop the death spiral.

You would rather be first than best, but you have to meet the competition's best over time, or you will lose your advantage. You must always remember that the consumer measures "better" and "best" in terms of the whole product.

Shrewd Competitors: Microsoft versus Apple

A different competition over product standards—between IBM and Microsoft on one side and Apple on the other—shows that shrewd competition can keep you from being "Betamaxed."

The story begins on a similar note. Again, the two standards were completely incompatible; PC users could not use Apple software or peripherals, and vice versa. Once again, the innovators did not realize the full potential of their inventions. None of the dozen or so early pioneers in desktop computing seems to have guessed how quickly every household in America (and indeed, worldwide) would want a desktop computer.

IBM's earliest PCs were designed to compete for the technological hobbyist market, such as ham radio operators or people who built cars from kits. Apple crafted their easier-to-use computers for a few specialized markets, including consumers who could afford a higher-end product. When a vast general market for desktops emerged, the two industry leaders were caught by surprise, but they offered very different products, each with distinct advantages and disadvantages. What followed is like a primer in shrewd competition.

IBM achieved market dominance almost by accident. The early PC was inexpensive to build, with an "open architecture" that other designers could easily add to. IBM embraced these partners and allowed other companies to write software or build peripherals for their machines. This meant a huge advantage in price and availability of allied products for the IBM machines and the clones that followed, all of which ran the MS-DOS operating system that was developed for IBM by a little company called Microsoft (the MS in MS-DOS).

Apple's advantages were a mix of convenience and quality. Apple's mouse-driven graphic operating system was far more user-friendly than MS-DOS. Early adopters found they could do more things more easily on their Apples, particularly when it came to graphics. However, with many more hardware and software developers working on products for PCs, this advantage steadily eroded. What was already easy on an Apple remained easier to do, but soon working with a PC became easier as well.

However, neither company ever developed a decisive advantage that could wipe out the other. By the time Microsoft had developed a competitive version of Apple's operating system, which it called Windows, Apple machines had worked with the manufacturers of widely used software applications to create Apple-friendly versions. Although Apple computers, peripherals, and software remained relatively more expensive, Apple remains in complete control of a few key high-paying markets in the education field and industries like advertising and publishing. (This strategy, called vertical marketing, will be discussed later.) Apple's dominance of product placement in entertainment has had a comical side effect: although the vast majority of Americans use Windows computers, the vast majority of characters in American movies and television shows use Apples.

And it's no longer a head-to-head competition, as Apple has prudently branched out into other product lines, such as the iPod.

This is how the big boys benchmark against the competition. Learn from them, and ask yourself:

- How closely can I copy what my competitors are currently doing better than I am?
- What can I do that they aren't doing at all?
- What will it cost me to make these changes?

If you search hard enough, you can find your advantage, and a portion of the market to support you.

If You Can't Beat Them, Join Them

Sometimes you can make the competition a partner. For example, I am not an expert at baking cookies. I only know how to make brownies. If I were to add cookies to my product line, I'd probably arrange to resell Mrs. Fields or Otis Spunkmeyer cookies, the same way I resell flowers and balloons. The profit margin would be lower than if I could make cookies from scratch—but the profit margin from having people cross the street to buy Mrs. Fields cookies instead of mine would be zero.

Stick with what you know. Don't try to do everything. Try to concentrate on the things no competitor does better—and do them right.

If You Can Beat Them, Beat Them Hard

When I checked out my own competition, I found that they were printing various kinds of customer materials. I ordered their literature and signed up for their e-mail blasts.

Then I outdid them. At one point, I was printing all of the following materials:

- *Brownie Points coupons.* This loyalty program enables customers to receive free delivery by submitting feedback about their experiences with Luv's Brownies®.

- *Gift cards*. I attached gift cards to each gift package sold.
- *Postcards*. I printed custom-designed cards for bridal fairs.
- *More postcards*. I also prepared cards for holidays such as Valentine's Day.
- *Brochures*. My brochures were lengthy—up to 10 pages.
- *Special notes*. I affixed notes spelling out the shelf life of perishable items to every shipping box.
- *Customer satisfaction postcards*. This was another chance to get feedback about orders.

But of course, you have to benchmark costs as well. With more and more people using computers and e-mail, I've been able to save money by doing most of my printing to Adobe Acrobat files (PDFs). I used to print thousands of brochures; now, I use an electronic format and e-mail my materials to customers. E-mail isn't just cheaper than using the post office—it's faster, too.

Any time you can do more than the competition and spend less money doing it, you are on top of your game.

Who Are Your Best Customers?

This is a trick question. I'm not looking for a demographic answer, like "The best customers are young people aged 18-25 years because they decide what is cutting-edge and set trends," or "The best customers are higher-income white-collar professionals, because they have more money to spend." No, the answer is far simpler—your best customers are *the ones you already have*.

There's a rule of thumb called the 80/20 rule (also known as the Pareto Principle). Management theorist Joseph Juran formulated it in the 1930s based on observations made by economist Vilfredo Pareto, who noted that 80 percent of the income in Italy was distributed among 20 percent of the people. The 80/20 rule states that in a given situation where the actions of independent units create a result, you can expect that 80 percent of the result is caused by 20 percent of the units. The 80/20 rule isn't a law of nature, but it's usually a good first estimate, and it reveals that over a period of time, 80 percent of your sales are likely to come from 20 percent of your customers—your repeat customers, the same customers you have now.

There are three more things you have to understand about your current customers and their value to you:

It is much cheaper to keep them than to acquire new customers. Why? To get new customers you have to advertise to a large population, and there's a realistic likelihood that most consumers will not respond, and only a small percentage will come into your store. Your current customers already know who you are and what products or services you provide. They're already sold on you. Although I do suggest that you spend a little money on them in the form of loyalty and incentive programs, this is a much more efficient use of your marketing dollar—because not one penny will be aimed at nonresponders.

You will save advertising money by focusing on your current customers, because they are actually walking advertisements for you. Think about your own habits. We all like to talk about our favorite goods and services. "You think that's good music? Listen to this!" "Yes, and I got it for a terrific sale price at the store on the corner, which has great clothes!" When a friend tells you a sob story about how badly he was treated by a company, you can hardly wait to butt in and say, "You don't want to get your technical support from Jones. Believe me, I am completely familiar with this market; I've tried Jones, and Doe, and Brown, and they've all let me down. A couple of years ago, my accountant told me about Smith, and sure enough, Smith is terrific." People love to help their friends find a better product and show off their knowledge about quality; they are ready and willing to give you the best advertising of all—word of mouth—if you treat them right. If you send loyal customers a coupon entitling both them and a friend to 20 percent off a purchase if they make a referral, you've given them a reason to share their knowledge about your business.

When you lose a customer, the reason why that happened will spread by word of mouth, too. You never lose just one customer when you make her unhappy. You lose every potential customer that she talks to about you. Again, consider how you feel as a consumer when you ask your friends where you should go for a certain product or service. If a buddy tells you he has had a good experience with a company, that makes a positive impression, and if 10 people tell you the same thing, you're almost sold. But if the eleventh person tells you a horror story about poor quality, nondelivery, or rude customer support staff, that pretty much cancels out the 10 good reports. So both the customer you keep and the customer you drive away will talk about you, and they will both be listened to—but remember that the negative stories always register more strongly.

Loyalty and Incentive Programs

Once you understand that your best customers are the ones you already have, how do you keep them? Treat them well and offer them incentives to stay with you and expand their use of your services. For instance, in exchange for customer feedback my company offers "Brownie Points" that are redeemable for free delivery or shipping. This is a great incentive for repeat customers.

Be creative with loyalty programs such as freebies, discounts, and contests. They really work. A friend once took me to a sports bar and grill that would stamp your customer card for every submarine sandwich you ordered. You had to fill the whole card—12 stamps—to get a free sandwich, but the cards were a convenient size to carry and had some useful sports-schedule information on the other side. The promise of eventually getting a free sandwich kept everyone coming back, and soon the bar was also offering a small prize to the first customer to fill in *six* cards. Imagine the repeat business it got as people competed to be its best customers!

If you assess your advertising and marketing budget on a per-customer basis, you'll find that the costs of incentive programs average much less than the cost of acquiring brand new customers.

A Little Neighborhood Luv

Reach out to your neighborhood. Local customers make terrific repeat customers. One good way to reach them is through "Welcome to the Neighborhood" or similar direct-mail postcards. The companies that create them target specific zip codes and develop the seasonal greetings for you.

Consider joining your local chamber of commerce. Depending on the town you live in, chambers of commerce offer various services for small businesses. See if you can get access to the chamber's mailing list to create direct-mail campaigns and promotional offers. You may be able to use office space at the chamber to interview new employees or handle other meetings that your virtual office can't accommodate. Throw a monthly mixer for your fellow chamber members—they make great customers and business partners.

I once sold Valentine's Day gifts to my fellow chamber members and used the chamber's office space as the place where they could pick up their orders. It was convenient for them, and of course much more so for me—I didn't have to drive all over the city delivering brownies.

Schools and colleges. I previously discussed the advantages of partnering with charities and community groups. Schools and colleges will provide you with additional opportunities to develop a local market. My home base in the San Francisco Bay Area is rich in colleges. When the dot-com and other high-tech industries slowed down and began to lay off workers a few years ago, student enrollment levels rose, and I decided to go where the customers were.

One junior college started a "student-to-business" program, which was a way for local businesses to meet and greet the kids on campus. Small businesses were welcome to sell their products, offer discounts or incentives, advertise in the newspaper at a promotional rate, and take advantage of many other integrated marketing-communications activities. I sold books and brownies and made appearances as a paid speaker. College students love snacks, so my business was particularly well suited to the program, but quite a large range of other businesses were successful as well.

Partner with a Neighborhood Business

Once you establish a good relationship with a local channel partner, it may begin to share its customer base with you.

I've already mentioned the grocery stores that I partnered with early in my business's development. I sold my Luv Bites® (bite-sized heart-shaped brownies) through a local grocery store and deli, Zanotto's. Because these bite-sized heart-shaped brownies weren't pre-wrapped when I delivered them, the deli customer didn't know they weren't made in-house. They were popular, and the store appreciated that, so for Valentine's Day it pumped up my business with a big promotion: it featured Luv's Brownies® as its premiere Valentine's Day gift.

I developed a personal relationship with the wonderful Zanotto family. They sold my entire product line, and eventually allowed me to come into the store and bake fresh brownies on the premises for customers. I had instant access to a family-like relationship with a local customer base the store had built up over many years.

Your best customers come back because you feel like family. Treat them that way. Show them the sort of support, hand-holding, and communication you'd show a younger sister or brother.

Support—First, Last, and Always

What's the most important way to show love for your family? By showing constant, unwavering support. Your family members know that you are always there to listen to their problems and do what you can, even if it is only to offer sympathy and encouragement.

Your customers want the same thing—and they're paying for it.

Customer support is one of the biggest issues in corporate management. Every business knows how important it is, but time after time, major companies score terrible marks in customer satisfaction surveys. The problem is simple: good customer support is worker- and labor-intensive. Companies often respond to the personnel demand by making support a low-paying, entry-level position, or by outsourcing it. Unfortunately, this is not an area where you can cut corners without the customer noticing.

Once a company is beyond a certain size and complexity, customer service is almost the only part of the company—other than its products—that the customer sees. Customer support coordinators give presale information about products and prices; they take and process the orders; they respond to quality or delivery problems; and they may even have to explain how to use the product after it arrives. To the customer, the voice at the other end of the customer support line *is* the company.

Earlier, I discussed how important repeatable processes are to implementing effective customer support. The right processes help ensure that the order will be taken correctly, and that many common ordering and delivery mistakes that irritate customers won't happen in the first place. But when mistakes happen anyway—you can never prevent them all—there should also be a process in place for smoothly escalating a customer complaint up the line to a manager, or maybe you, who can handle it to the customer's satisfaction.

There's more to customer support than procedures. Attitude is all-important. It is vital that you—or a training specialist—thoroughly instruct your customer support staff about courtesy, cheerfulness, and proactive attention. This training must be periodically refreshed. The best workers in the world face a slow degradation in morale when they do the same thing day after day. They must be reminded that in business, cheerfulness is not an emotion but a habit; if you can fake it when you don't feel it, soon you aren't faking it at all.

Always listen to your support staff as they do their jobs, and put yourself in the customer's shoes as you do so. If necessary, take some calls yourself to show your team how it should be done. Set a good example when you deal with customers, both when the customer is in front of you and after he is gone. Don't make a play for popularity by displaying an us-versus-them attitude about the customers. Remarks like "Wasn't she cranky?" or "What an obnoxious voice!" don't benefit your business, and you certainly don't want other customers hearing them.

Of course, you will eventually get an occasional offensive or even crazy customer, and it's important to let your staff know that you will support them if they behave well in situations when the customer simply cannot be satisfied. Aside from these few exceptional situations, however, never speak negatively about customers in front of your staff. You want them to feel that all the customers are your friends, and that if they ignore, neglect, or offend a customer, doing so is just as wrong as doing the same thing to you.

Hand-holding

There are other ways in which the customer relationship is like a family relationship. Families often go through big changes, and not all members of the family find this easy to manage. For instance, when a new baby arrives, her older brother may have problems dealing with the fact that everyone is thinking and talking about the newcomer. The focus of attention has changed, and the brother may feel that he is not considered as important as before, and that he is being neglected. If this happened in your family, you would certainly make an effort to show special attention to the worried child. You would hold his hand, talk about his concerns, make him feel that he is as well-loved as ever, and assure him that everything is all right.

Life lessons are business lessons, and business lessons are life lessons.

It is a very exciting time in your small business's life when you make it bigger. You may introduce a new product line, or a whole different way of servicing your customers. You're very proud of it, you're exhausted from the effort of making it happen, and you can't help but be particularly interested in the impression that it is going to make on *new* customers, who are blissfully unaware of the old way of doing things at your business.

At a time like this, it is crucially important to not neglect your existing customers. Don't be surprised if they need hand-holding. Communicate with them personally. Make sure they understand the new product or procedure; specifically, make sure they understand that the change will be an improvement for *them*. Customers are also emotionally conservative. They came to you because they liked the product or service you had *then*; any change you make has the potential of throwing the whole relationship into question. But like the child in the previous example, customers mainly want reassurance that you haven't forgotten about them and still care about them. The exact details aren't important. They just want you to hold their hands and personally walk them through the new deal; if you do, they will usually buy into it.

Communication

Hand-holding is just one example of the constant communication that keeps a family together. If you want to keep your customers, make sure they feel that you are always talking to them and that they can talk to you whenever they wish.

The simplest version of this sort of communication is the customer survey; it's simple to implement and simple to follow up on. Make sure your customer has a chance to comment on every transaction with your business. It doesn't matter if the comment is negative or positive—it is always very valuable to you.

Negative comments enable you to catch serious problems before they cost you customers. If a customer is about to blow you off forever, she will not take the time to fill in the customer satisfaction form you've included with the order. The fact that she did fill it in—no matter how negative the comment was—tells you that she still has a little faith or hope that you will correct the problem she is reporting and she'll be able to continue being your customer. Try to always make a personal response to every negative comment, even if it's just an apology and a promise to do better next time. If you do, you can usually keep the customer, because you've proven you care about her personally.

Of course, positive comments are always a pleasure. I can't help sharing a few examples I've received in the past:

- "Excellent brownies and service. I've done business with this company for years and have always had a great experience."—*James Gordon*

- "The service was great! The birthday brownie was delivered to our son on the day of his birthday with a candle. He and his college friends said the brownie was awesome! Ordering from this company was a breeze."
  —*Wanda Smith*
- "Aundrea goes above and beyond to make sure her quality products are beautifully presented. Her personal touch makes all the difference!"—*Sandi Nelson*

Customer feedback like this doesn't just make you feel good and tell you what you are doing right—it cements a relationship. A customer may have a vague feeling that he likes what you do, but when he takes the time to put it into words and send it to you, it becomes more important and personal to him, and fixed in his mind. Don't pass up the chance to personally respond to some of the positive comments as well—it's usually a pleasure, you might make a new friend, and it can give you a customer for life.

You should also communicate proactively. Try to give your regular customers advance word of changes or new items as part of your loyalty programs. Let them know they're on the inside track. And if you have a few big customers who carry a large part of your business, make sure you have positive personal relationships with them. When you have a bit of news for them, call them, and always use the opportunity to ask if there are any problems they've been having with your service, or if there's anything you can do to make them more satisfied. You should never take a customer for granted.

The Right Kind of Family

It's strange and hard to understand, but you can see it happening every day in families all around you. Many people have a tendency to take their closest loved ones for granted.

Perhaps the logic is that if you're going to exhibit bad behavior somewhere, you should do so with your sister, your mother-in-law, or even your spouse, because they know you really love them and your relationships with them are stronger than any one foolish choice you might make. Sometimes we don't just shortchange the ones we love—we actually take our frustrations out on them. Treating the boss or the IRS auditor or the traffic cop badly would have negative consequences, so we dump our bad feelings on those closest to us because they're available and because we think we can count on them to know we "don't really mean it."

People who behave this way in their personal relationships find it easy to carry over similar behaviors into their customer relationships. If you've fallen behind in deliveries and are left to choose one delivery to make late and one to make on time, it's tempting to say, "Well, Mr. Jones is a new customer. I want to impress him and can't afford to irritate him. Mrs. Smith is a reliable customer, and she will understand if she gets her stuff late this one time; we have an existing relationship." If it's truly only a one-time thing, that logic might even make sense. But once you start thinking that way, there's a tendency to keep doing it and to neglect the customers you should value the most—your regulars.

Bad behavior is bad behavior. If you neglect or abuse those closest to you—no matter how good the underlying relationship was—you may be headed for breakup, divorce, or never speaking to one another again. Meanwhile, your business customers were *never* as close to you as your nearest and dearest; they will quite rightly bail out on you the first time another supplier comes around asking, "Is your current supplier really treating you like a valued customer?"

The moral is, don't just treat your regular customers as if they were family. Treat them as members of an *ideal* family; treat them the way you *wish* every member of your family treated you, all the time.

Targeting Vertical Markets

One day, I sat at work thinking about how multibillion-dollar companies made their money in such diverse ways. My own small business was suffering from two problems, neither of which was my fault.

My local market happened to consist of America's biggest high-tech and computing sector, and at that moment it was in the middle of a total industry meltdown. That meant less money for local consumers to spend on luxuries, like brownies. On top of that, the country as a whole had begun a love affair with low-carbohydrate diets, and many consumers making that transition assumed that brownies didn't fit the diet.

I needed to reinvent my business and seek out uncharted waters. I asked myself what the high-tech businesses I had worked in would do, and the answer was:

- Segmentation
- Targeting
- Vertical marketing

These three marketing terms are related.

Segmentation is the process of analyzing a market and dividing it into segments that have common consumer needs and desires. If you make cars and trucks, for instance, your market includes both family heads and young singles, but they have very different needs and desires when it comes to what they drive. You can sell to both groups, but you'll do so separately, pushing different vehicle types to each; the two groups represent separate segments of your total market.

Targeting is what you can do after you understand the segmentation of your market: you'll be able to position your product, or different parts of your product line, in a way that emphasizes the appeal to each targeted segment.

Vertical marketing represents a special case of segmentation and targeting. Sometimes you'll recognize that a segment of your larger market is an entire industry or specialized organization, which gives you an opportunity to isolate the target and capture it whole. Earlier, I described how Apple held its own against IBM and Microsoft by capturing vertical markets in the education and entertainment industries. Provide an industry with a customized turnkey solution to its problems, and it will become so tied to your specific products and services that it will actively resist your competitors.

I decided to apply these tools to my market problem.

The First Step: Marshal Your Full Line of Products

I had to get past the idea that I only had one product; that's too inflexible a position from which to target multiple segments. This is when I started seeing Luv's Brownies® in terms of my Three Bs:

- *Bakery*. Retail and online sales.
- *Book*. Sales, readings, and signings.
- *Baby*. I am executing my plan to recreate and sell my childhood doll Luv.

This is my childhood doll, Luv. My parents gave her to me as a Christmas gift when I was three years old.

I determined to push all my products in an integrated fashion. Whether I was at a bridal fair, chocolate festival, grocery-store baking demonstration, or any other face-to-face interaction with customers, I tried to bake and sell fresh brownies on site, sell my book, and let people know I was available for readings or signings. When the time comes, I will sell my Luv doll alongside the books and brownies.

The Second Step: Segment and Target Vertical Markets

What vertical markets could I hope to penetrate with my brownies, my book, and my speaking engagements? How would I position myself to target them? I settled on four.

Education. The venues I chose were junior colleges, libraries, and universities. The key message I selected for this group was, "Don't let any challenge stop you from making your dreams a reality." In the San Francisco Bay Area, there are more than 30 colleges. The San Jose/Silicon Valley area has 10 more. Because I was born and raised in the Bay Area, a student at quite a few of the junior colleges, and a graduate of San Jose State and Golden Gate University in San Francisco, I could see hooks to get my products into the educational system. During Black History Month and Women's History Month, students could buy my brownies for fund-raisers, gift fairs, and Valentine's Day celebrations. I could sell books at the university bookstore, and I could sell both books and brownies at university events. Schools could pay me to speak about challenges in school, life, and business.

Financial. I decided to approach financial organizations like Wells Fargo Bank, some mortgage brokers, and some wholesalers. The key message I selected for this group was, "Home is where the heart is." Members of this group are always looking for a way to thank clients, but they generally prefer to spend no more than $25 because that is the maximum they are allowed to write off. For the San Francisco Bay Area, I could develop a $25 custom package to celebrate home loan approvals with brownies and balloons. This combination has become one of my hottest sellers. Through the contacts it has made for me, I have obtained the opportunity to speak at real estate boards' monthly meetings and sell books to folks who are just getting started in business and want to know more about how to market themselves.

Healthcare. In particular, I decided to target heart surgeons, hospitals, wellness fairs, activities for persons with diabetes, and AIDS-awareness groups and events. The key message I selected for this group was, "Brownies always bring a smile from the heart." This can be a tough area to break into, but I'd made a lot of contacts in healthcare while dealing with James's illness; I'd met quite a few doctors and patients who'd asked me to make someone's day with brownies. To capture the diabetic market, I have donated sugar-free brownies to America's Diabetic Walk and the Silicon Valley Diabetic Association.

Retail. I decided to go after niche grocery stores, neighborhood grocery stores, and small bakeries that mainly make bread or that don't want to take on baking a new product. The key message I selected for this group to pass along to their customers was, "Moderation is the key to a healthy lifestyle." In California, it has been challenging to keep my business afloat with so many people watching what they eat. But it isn't what you eat—it's how much. I decided to take on the low-carb movement and push moderation. Niche grocery stores, neighborhood stores, and small bakeries could choose to sell my product, which is delivered each morning, as a turnkey solution—they'd be able to sell fresh-baked brownies from scratch, but they wouldn't have to make them, and they'd only have to pay for what they sold.

The Third Step: A SWOT Analysis

But how could I judge whether any of these efforts would be successful in advance? Where would I stand relative to possible competitors like Mrs. Fields, Famous Amos, and half a dozen others? I decided to use another marketing tool I'd picked up in the high-tech world: the Strengths/Weaknesses/Opportunities/Threats (SWOT) analysis.

- *Strengths*. I knew the local markets well enough to target them very specifically. I had enough business background to employ an integrated marketing communications (marcom) approach.
- *Weaknesses*. It might be hard to fully staff some of the events unless I'd be gearing up for a big holiday.
- *Opportunities*. No other competitors were offering fresh-baked brownies or gift baskets *and* balloons *and* roses, delivered. No other competitor seemed to have segmented these markets for vertical penetration.
- *Threats*. In the education segment, I'd be competing with the onsite cafeteria and other vendors; price breaks might be hard to give when the education market already gets such a large discount. Big competitors with economies of scale, such as Mrs. Fields, could come in and undercut me by 50 percent. But that would be the case only if they recognized the opportunity.

My SWOT analysis told me that my competitors didn't have a vertical strategy and therefore wouldn't have an integrated marcom campaign to oppose me. I should grab the opportunity.

The Fourth Step: The Integrated Marketing Communications (Marcom) Plan

Your business plan is your marketing plan. When you are looking at a targeted segment—whether it's a whole vertical market or one trade show—define a "go to market" strategy that involves every aspect of your business. I knew the demographics for my local market—age groups, ethnicity, and so forth—but I soon realized that it was more important to concentrate on psychographics, which is a term that describes data about lifestyles.

For each vertical market, I reviewed my psychographics research and laid out an integrated marcom plan of specifically targeted campaigns by following a standard procedure:

- Define the audience
- Define the message
- Create deliverables (brochures, gift tags, personalized packaging, special packaging, and so forth)
- Develop a calendar of events
- Measure the results and tweak as needed

Naturally, this resulted in different campaigns for each vertical market. I put together the following list for the education segment:

1. The student lifestyle searches for convenience and flexibility to face the challenges of classes and studying. My events must fit both a student budget and a student schedule.
2. My event calendar should be built around the dates of speaking engagements; events that suited promotional events for my book, like Black History Month or Women's History Month; and holidays for which brownies and balloons are a good fit.
3. My marcom plan would include stories or announcements in the school paper, an e-mail blast to instructors, my event listed on websites, flyers handed out on campus, and brownies and other deliverables at every book signing.

The financial market campaign was even more psychographically driven than the education campaign. The psychographics values for real estate agents were:

- Value independence
- Assertive and driven personalities
- Focus on building and maintaining relationships

Because agents are born networkers, their meaningful relationships include everything from friends, neighbors, and family to schools, churches, community groups, and banks. Key words in messages to this group would include "warm," "chocolate," "memorable," "unique," and "customized." Key phrases would include "more personal than a card" and "more desirable than flowers."

For the financial sector, I implemented a "push" strategy—that is, a promotion that builds awareness of the product and pushes customers into action. I already had real estate agents buying baskets for their clients as appreciation gifts. Now those baskets would include 20-percent-off coupons that the recipients could use to place new orders for themselves. I figured I would spend $5,000 on the promotion and then measure the coupons redeemed and the total revenue I'd received. If the net was $10,000, I'd have a 50 percent ROI.

This strategy included direct mail and e-mail communication with cause marketing. What is cause marketing? If an agent bought a $25.00 real estate package, I would donate $1.25 to their agency's charity. For example:

- Century 21 donates to Easter Seals and The College Fund
- Coldwell Banker donates to Habitat for Humanity
- ERA donates to Muscular Dystrophy

My total push included a sponsorship campaign. I would attend:

- The National Association of Realtors Expo
- American Real Estate Society Meetings
- Bay Area Real Estate meetings

My personal selling and public relations were not limited to these meetings. I also:

- attended open houses and dropped off brownies
- subscribed to an industry newsletter
- made personal visits to real estate offices
- created awards for my best partners
- became a featured speaker at relevant events
- scheduled two to three business lunches per week

- had contractors drop off samples and literature to new real estate agents
- continually sought stories in printed publications

Relationship-building is the key to success in vertical marketing. If you can really bond with the customer, you can keep the competition out. I made a special effort for the financial vertical market because they are such great networkers. They spread my message for me. The value of everything I put into this vertical market was multiplied accordingly.

When It All Comes Together

It seemed like only a few months had passed since the economic downturn and a dietary fad had negatively affected my business. But because I'd spent time exploring the possibilities of vertical markets, I had rising sales from a new set of customers that most people would never associate with my product. What do brownies have to do with education or real estate? My small business was successfully fishing in new waters because I'd asked myself what a multibillion-dollar company would do.

Study the winners and you'll learn how to win.

Free Media Exposure

It isn't easy to get free exposure in the media anymore—or at least, it's not as easy as it was during the dot-com boom of the late 1990s. During the boom, companies weren't asked hard questions like, "Do you have customers? Do you have a business plan?" Pitches were high-concept. Twenty-year-old CEOs confidently said that they could spin straw into gold, and business reporters would faithfully repeat their boasts and fantasies.

When I was pursuing my undergraduate degree, I took a marketing course in brand management. I learned that your brand is your promise to the people who use your product or service, and that it is the promise they remember you by. Many shiny start-ups broke their promises a decade ago, and no one remembers them today.

I knew that for Luv's Brownies®, I had to go back to marketing communication basics to get my message out at minimal cost.

A former colleague named Scott created my Luv's Brownies® and Luv Bites® logos. I hired a small creative agency to design my company stationery, folders, labels, postcards, gift cards, business cards, and website. I wanted to make sure all of my deliverables looked alike and reflected a fun brand that promises delicious brownies for everyone. When you present a consistent design, every transaction you have with a customer is like a free advertisement.

While my literature and website were being created, I worked on my unique selling proposition. I've heard unique selling propositions referred to as "elevator pitches", and I think that's an apt description—it's a few sentences or a catch-phrase you can deliver in the brief time you share with someone between floors. Soon, whenever a reporter asked me what Luv's Brownies® was or what made it different, I had my answer: "Home of the Original Heart-Shaped Brownie®."

Once I knew that my unique selling proposition was effective, I began to assemble a press kit for media outlets. I was working in the high-tech field at the time, so I picked up a press kit at each and every computer company I visited. I studied and compared them and tried to determine what worked and what didn't. Then I created my own press kit and sent it directly to San Jose State University, *Golden Gate University* magazine, and local newspapers and TV shows. I wanted to start out small and locally and then hit the bigger news outlets. Within weeks, I got a few calls from local newspapers and TV programs. My press kits had worked! Immediately, I started to get stories in print and online publications because of the hooks I'd supplied:

- I was born and raised in the San Francisco Bay Area. One headline read, "Local Girl Bakes Good."
- I created the brownie recipe by accident, because of dyslexia, and named it after my childhood doll named Luv.

The headline for a story with that focus read, "Brownie Baker Puts Lots of Luv in the Oven."

- I was simultaneously working in the high-tech industry and moonlighting as a brownie baker. That hook led to a piece entitled "A Day in the Life," and inspired another magazine to put its own spin on the story: "Recipe 'Mistake' Leads Rose Garden Woman to Secret Brownie Business Success."

Once your story is out there, other feature writers read it and supply their own hooks.

- One local newspaper had an article on the disappearance of the small bakery, which of course was caused by the onslaught of grocery store and big-box store bakeries. The article's other focus was the fad of online bakeries. The article's title? "Baking for Bucks."
- Another newspaper did a story on spicing up your partner's life with little surprises and featured Luv's Brownies® in the Love and Romance section.

An online bakery can sell nationally, but for three years, I honed my message to customers in the San Francisco Bay Area media market. I had to get a handle on what I wanted to communicate about each of my product lines: heart-shaped brownie cakes, mail-order gifts, and wedding favors.

Message refinement turned out to be a constant battle. I realized that I needed to be really clear as I communicated information about my product lines. One magazine article implied that my brownie recipe included milk, which is not true. The same article also failed to mention that I offer a line of sugar-free brownies sweetened with Equal.

Here were the messages I worked to put across:

- *Heart-shaped brownie cakes* are only available for delivery in the San Francisco Bay Area. These cakes make a perfect customized gift for Valentine's Day, Mother's Day, Father's Day, birthdays, anniversaries, and company parties, but they cannot be shipped via FedEx. The cakes are decorated with butter cream frosting, which doesn't ship well and gets all over the inside of the box. For now, brownie cakes are only available locally.

- *Mail-order gifts* include brownie gift baskets and gift tins or coffee mugs filled with Luv Bites®. These products *can* be shipped via FedEx and delivered throughout the United States. Unfortunately, some reporters assumed that since I used FedEx, I was shipping worldwide, and one story that made that claim resulted in tens of thousands of e-mails and inquiries from overseas. Because I do not use preservatives, I can't ship worldwide. Eventually, I was able to communicate the delivery message through the ordering process: A visitor to the Luv's Brownies® website sees different choices depending on where he wants the gift shipped. If the shipping destination is in the San Francisco Bay area, he'd be able to order the entire product line, but he wouldn't be able to choose cakes or certain wedding favors if he were shipping to Atlanta.

- *Wedding favors* seemed to confuse customers the most. Depending on whether or not they use butter cream frosting, some favors can be shipped via FedEx across country and others are only available for delivery in the Bay Area. The 4-inch custom-decorated brownie cannot be shipped and Luv Bites® can, but they're both wedding favors. Someone suggested I put the decorated 4-inch brownie in the brownie cake section for consistency's sake. It seemed like a good idea, but in practice, most customers didn't understand it. How can a 4-inch brownie be a cake? This led to endless questions about bigger or personalized favors. So I worked out my current system as the result of customer feedback.

Once I knew I had a clear message about my product line and delivery process, I was ready to hit the New York press. I created a press kit that included the following:

- Articles from the *San Jose Mercury News*, *San Jose Magazine*, *Silicon Valley Inc.*, and others
- High-resolution versions of my picture, Luv's picture, and brownie pictures on CD
- My backgrounder, which includes my name, age, years in business, the year I started the business, number of employees, and so forth
- A company backgrounder and a list of fast facts about the business
- Customer testimonials
- A brochure including pricing and pictures
- A business card that included a URL for my online press center
- Details about the "Brownie Points" customer loyalty program

Within two weeks, *Essence* and *Black Enterprise* called me to do stories about my company.

But public relations is a continual process that is sometimes hit or miss. *Black Enterprise* first called me in 1998, and it did feature me on the cover—in November of 2006! During the first phone call, the reporter asked me some questions and asked me to keep in touch, and I did: I continued to send additional information for the next eight years. In 2004, I received a phone call from Jermine Benton, a *Black Enterprise* staff writer. She asked me a few more questions and sent me a questionnaire. During the next two years, the prospective story angle changed many times, and in the end, the would-be piece went from a magazine story to an online story to no story at all. When Jermine broke the news to me, I told her, "That's okay. Thank you for your time. Maybe another time, or another year. It was great speaking with you, and please keep in touch." It's nice to be featured in a story. But after all, I started this business because

I loved brownies and making people happy. It was never about becoming famous. I was in business for the long haul.

At my company's 10-year anniversary party, which was held in October 2006 at Jay-Z's 40/40 Club in New York, several staff members of *Black Enterprise* who were in attendance surprised me with the November 2006 issue—which featured me on the cover!

You shouldn't obsess about getting stories, but magazine, newspaper, and television reports lend credibility to your company. An advertisement in a magazine without a customer testimonial is just another ad. The news and feature stories between the ads are what consumers actually pay attention to, and that's what it's all about. If you have a good product or service, it will sell itself, and the press will follow.

Keep Current with Technology

When I worked and consulted in the high-tech field, I attended a lot of trade shows all over the world. I would always visit the press room or online press center for each show and continue my habit of collecting press kits for study and comparison. As time went on, I made changes to my own press kit to conform to the latest and greatest technology.

Instead of carrying all my content in a folder, I keep it on a flash memory stick. I can be anywhere in the world and still deliver my backgrounder, high-resolution photos, or any other information about my company by plugging that stick into a local computer. It can be displayed onscreen immediately or e-mailed to any reporter (or any number of reporters at different locations) via the Internet.

Whenever someone offers to do a story on your company, you want to be able to respond "in a flash."

The Art of Being Interviewed

Most of this discussion has concerned print media. But once you get your story out there, you will be given opportunities for radio or television exposure. Don't be shy about them. You may think

Earl G. Graves, Sr.
Chairman & Publisher

December 8, 2006

Ms. Aundrea Lacy
Luv's Brownies
2910 Stevens Creek Boulevard
#109
San Jose, CA 95128

Dear Aundrea,

On behalf of the entire BLACK ENTERPRISE family, I would like to extend my congratulations to you on being selected to appear on the cover our November 2006 issue. You are a symbol of success for black business owners and an inspiration to entrepreneurs looking to follow in your footsteps.

It is an honor to present you with this customized framed cover of our November 2006 issue. You are the quintessential business woman and BLACK ENTERPRISE is proud to recognize your accomplishments. Best wishes for continued success in all of your business pursuits.

Warmest Regards,

Earl

Earl G. Graves Publishing Co., Inc.
130 Fifth Avenue New York, New York 10011-4399
Tel: 212-886-9510 Fax 212-886-9532

Letter from Black Enterprise

you'll have stage fright, but most promotional interviews are actually a pleasant experience.

In a radio studio, you won't even have an audience to worry about—thousands may be listening (if you're lucky!), but you won't see them. You'll just be talking with the interviewer one-on-one, and she'll be easy to talk to—or she wouldn't be in that line of work.

In a television studio with a live audience, you'll be able to hear them, but you may not be able to see much, depending on the studio lighting. Even in this situation, you have nothing to worry about. The people who produce these shows know their business, and every step of the process is designed to keep you relaxed and at ease. You'll be prepared for the interview questions. If the director wants you to look at a certain camera, he will let you know, and he'll caution you not to stare directly into it. In most circumstances, that isn't even likely to come up, since you'll probably just be looking at the host in a natural way as you converse.

You have one job to do: always make sure you have something to say. The host's nightmare—especially on the radio—is silence, or "dead air." Saying nothing but "Yes," "No," and "I don't know" is just as bad. As I mentioned, you will have a chance to review the topics of conversation beforehand; just relax and answer the questions as you would to a friend.

- If you see a chance to get in a prepared answer or story, take it, but don't try to wedge it in where it doesn't make sense.
- Never start a story you can't wrap up within 30 seconds or so.
- Don't interrupt the interviewer. (I'm not kidding; I've seen it happen.)
- Don't let nervousness get the better of you and start talking too fast. Simply breathing normally will usually prevent that.

It's truly not that difficult or scary, and you'll probably get a chance to do a few local radio shows before you have to worry about a national audience. Don't let a little stage fright keep you from the pleasure of hanging out—however briefly—with one of your favorite celebrities.

I will always have the wonderful memory of talking with Montel Williams before my appearance. He told me about his own entrepreneurial activities, how he built his show, and how he produces his own content. After the taping, he walked me to the front door and shook my hand, let me take pictures, and told me how much he appreciated my appearance. I couldn't believe what I was hearing. I was so happy I was there that I didn't even know how to say, "Thank you."

Put Yourself in Print

So far, I've discussed media exposure in newspapers, magazines, radio, and TV. What's left? The object you're holding in your hand.

By writing a book, you can do more than promote your business—you can permanently expand it. As long as your book is related to your business, each can be used to market the other. You can sell the book on your company website. You can plug your business at every reading, signing, or speaking engagement that is related to your book.

What might you write about? Your business is you. Do you cook in your business? Do you sell kitchen utensils, or special foods for people with diabetes? You've probably created a number of your own recipes over the years—that could be a book. Do you sell equipment for a particular sport, hobby, craft, or type of repair? Then you're probably in a good position to tell beginners how to start using that equipment or supply master tips for experts—there's your book.

The easiest kind of book to sell is a how-to book written by an expert. It's almost impossible to start your own small business without learning how to solve problems that someone else will want to solve in the future. Did you take over a franchise? Then you know useful tips and pitfalls to avoid in franchising. Don't you think other people would benefit from knowing what you know?

Informational or how-to books lend themselves well to speaking engagements. Once you've written a book on digital photography, it's not hard to come up with a half-hour presentation on the subject that will leave listeners wanting more. You know they're interested in the subject, or they wouldn't have shown up; you'll be able to sell them your book on the spot. I've sold thousands of my own books at personal events.

If you don't think you have a full-length book in you, what about a booklet or pamphlet? Many useful subjects can be handled in 40 to 50 pages. A local printer can inexpensively print a simple booklet for you, and distribution is easy if you sell it through your website.

Any public library has a number of good books on self-publishing full-length books. I particularly recommend those by Dan Poynter. There are three primary options for self-publishing.

Traditional self-publishing. Traditional self-publishing involves putting up thousands of dollars in advance, and it takes a lot of planning and commitment to sell the books yourself. Don't think that bookstores will carry them, or that people will buy them just because they're on a shelf; expect to market and sell them yourself, and have a place to store them in the meantime.

Print-on-demand. Modern technology now offers attractive alternatives to traditional self-publishing. Print-on-demand (POD) publishers keep a computer file of your book's contents and only print it when an order comes in. There's no inventory to worry about or pay taxes on. There's no big print run you have to pay for in advance. In many cases, the publisher will take the orders and mail out the product. Best of all, some Internet POD publishers don't require any up-front money; they just take their cut from actual sales. But POD can be expensive, and the higher price of the book will discourage many people from buying it.

E-books. You don't even have to print the book at all. You can produce it as an e-book—a PDF file that anyone can read on a computer with the free application Acrobat Reader. It costs literally nothing to publish this way, and you can sell and "ship" (via e-mail or download) the book directly from your website.

Since an e-book costs nothing to produce or ship, you can even consider giving it away free. Why would you do that? Well, suppose a customer is surfing for information on flycasting. If your website that sells bait and tackle offers a 40-page e-book on the subject for free, why wouldn't he stick around and check your site out? It gives a whole new meaning to the words bait and tackle, doesn't it?

The best reference I've seen for self-publishing e-books is *How to Publish and Promote Online* by M.J. Rose and Angela Adair-Hoy (St. Martin's Griffin, 2001). Adair-Hoy also offers good information on POD at her self-publishing website, www.booklocker.com.

I've just scratched the surface of this subject. When you add free publishing to free media exposure, the range of possibilities is an entrepreneur's dream.

Paid Advertisements

Paid advertisements take up only a small part of my marketing budget. I hope to dispel some common myths about paid advertising and show you that the most efficient forms are not the most showy and expensive ones; in fact, the most expensive forms of paid advertisements might be worthless to a small-business entrepreneur.

The Biggest Myth

From the moment you start running your own business, you will be told to advertise, advertise, advertise. There is a widespread belief that the bigger the ad (a full page in a newspaper), or the bigger the audience (a prime-time television spot), the more potent its effect on your sales will be.

Nothing could be further from the truth.

Even big ad agencies will concede that the most effective ads are a) persistent and b) targeted. Once you understand these qualities, you can consider whether or not a one-shot ad has them.

Persistence or Repetition

Consumers are bombarded with hundreds, if not thousands, of advertisements a day, and they have become good at not seeing them.

Most people ignore the average advertisement the first time they see it, and the second, and the third. Only through persistent repetition is an ad likely to work its way into a consumer's consciousness.

Persistence is more important than size. Some of the most effective paid ads in the marketplace are ones that run week after week in the same place in the same publication. Through repetition, they sink in, and they're in front of the consumer on the particular day when she finally decides to stop putting off the purchase of a product and begins comparing brands.

I've said that most people ignore the average ad the first few times they see it. But not all ads are average.

The Importance of Targeting

Judge by your own experience. You're turning the pages of a magazine. Ad after ad flips by, and you hardly notice. Suddenly you stop and focus on one. Why? Because it's aimed directly at something you are interested in. You are its target.

Once, I decided to change the foundation makeup I wore. I searched in department stores and could not find a good foundation that matched my skin tone, because most of them were too ashy or too yellow. One day, I saw an ad for Revlon cosmetics that featured the actress Halle Berry. Before seeing that ad, I was unaware that Revlon made foundation for black women. After seeing that ad, I considered trying Revlon ColorStay® foundation. Ten years later, I'm still wearing Revlon ColorStay® foundation.

The more personal and specific the interest, and the more directly it is related to the real benefits of the product, the more impact the ad is likely to have.

Re-examining the Big Ad

Now you can see that full-page advertisements and prime-time television commercials can be a complete waste of time for a small business if you don't have the right answers to the right questions.

- *Are they persistent?* Only if you have big bucks to keep running the ad again and again, and you probably don't.
- *Are they targeted?* That depends on how well you've crafted them.

But if you correctly target the narrow segment of the market that will be highly motivated to buy your product, why waste money showing the ad to hundreds of thousands of other people who couldn't care less? That's like renting a jumbo jet to take your two kids on a trip. And you probably won't even reach most of the segment you're targeting if you can only afford to run the ad once; if your targeted customers aren't watching that channel at that exact moment, your chance to reach them is gone.

Am I saying that TV commercials and full-page ads are worthless? That's obviously not true, or they wouldn't be so expensive. Television is the most effective ad medium of all, but only if you can afford to use it persistently. So until your business reaches a size that can command that sort of ad budget, let it go.

What Didn't Work, and What Did

I learned the big-ad lesson the hard way. It was Mother's Day 1997, and my product was still very new. I took out a single ad in a local newspaper that presented brownies, roses, and balloons as the ideal gift for Mom. It was a waste of $5,000. Today, I can think of at least four ways I could have made that ad much more effective—but it still wouldn't have been worth it.

For Father's Day, I reconsidered my advertising blunder and created a flyer. The flyer included:

- A coupon for 20 percent off
- Brownie Points for free delivery if customer feedback was provided
- A strong customer testimonial ("Best brownie I have ever tasted!")

- An invitation to meet me and watch me bake fresh brownies in a grocery-store partner's location

I arranged for my grocery-store partner to add the flyer information to its website, tuck the flyers into the store's weekly ads that were home-delivered locally, and drop the flyers into customers' bags. I featured the store appearance on my own website, sent an e-mail blast throughout the San Francisco Bay Area, and asked some of my friends to e-mail their friends about the promotion.

I sent out 200 flyers and received about 70 orders—far more than I got from the big newspaper ad. I had only been in business for seven months. This was the beginning of my education in real-world advertising.

The Full Range of Paid Ads

To most people, the phrase "paid advertisement" suggests TV and radio spots, magazine and newspaper ads, and billboards, and that's it. But if you think about it, you also advertise with smaller media: direct mail and e-mail, flyers, brochures, postcards, business cards, printed pens, balloons, coffee mugs, and many other items that you might pay to produce. For a small-business entrepreneur, the low-end deliverables are a far more efficient use of an advertising dollar. They can be coordinated to work together in an integrated marcom campaign. The net result: highly effective targeting.

Let me give you a few examples.

When even smaller is better. Because I run an Internet business, without a brick-and-mortar shop people can walk into, I like to meet customers directly at events like bridal shows. Do I hand out brochures? No, I give them much smaller customer cards that include a unique Internet URL that can link the customer to a website or page full of customized content that is designed for the specific audience of that particular show. That Web page can actually convey more information than any brochure for significantly less. A full-color brochure can cost you anywhere from $2.00 to

$5.00 each, but business cards only cost about $0.20 each when ordered by the thousand.

Speaking of cards, the humble business card is underrated and underused as a form of paid advertisement. Both sides can be printed: you can add a photograph of your goods or a map to your store. I use the back of my business card in two ways. It displays the unique URL of my online press center and offers Brownie Points, which can be redeemed for free delivery in the San Francisco Bay area, or free postage on mail-order items.

Because of their small size, cards are also more persistent than a brochure or flyer. Most people who are handed a flyer on the street throw it away as quickly as they possibly can. Business cards have a way of sticking around in pockets and purses and desk drawers for a much longer time. If you post a flyer on a bulletin board, it will probably be tossed out within a week, but business cards stuck in the bulletin board's frame often hang on until someone is interested enough to take them.

Making flyers fly. Flyers don't have to be disposable. As with every other bit of your literature and collateral, the goal is to get it working with your other marketing vectors in an integrated marcom campaign. A coupon on a flyer makes it a lot less likely to be thrown away. Many consumers like coupons that are redeemable online even better. You might also consider trying out two different approaches on flyers; if you have two different flyers with different coupons, you can measure which kind of coupon is getting back to the store more often, and that's direct feedback about which kind of flyer is more effective. Think of the flyer as a multipurpose marketing tool instead of "just a flyer."

Targeting direct mail. During the Internet boom of the late 1990s, direct-mail advertising almost died. E-mail was much cheaper to send and seemed to be the wave of the future. In 2004, new antispam laws cracked down on companies that sent unsolicited e-mail and gave direct-mail renewed appeal to businesses. It can be expensive unless it is well targeted, but a coordinated marcom approach will sharpen your targeting.

For example, I like to send a direct mail piece before a bridal show. The postcard will include:

- Time/date/place information about the show
- A coupon for a free brownie
- A discount for onsite orders of wedding favors
- An announcement of a fishbowl raffle for wedding favors. ("Just drop your postcard in the bowl.")

From the names I collect at the show, I can refine my direct-mail list into three kinds of leads, worth varying amounts of effort:

- *The A lead has expressed a strong interest in my product.* She has left a credit-card deposit or has paid in full, and has taken a business card. She appears to be the decision maker, has sampled the brownies, and has indicated that the product is a perfect fit for her wedding.
- *The B lead has expressed some interest.* He has taken a card, may have left a partial payment, may or may not be the decision maker but appears to have influence, and has sampled the brownies. He is probably still considering other products.
- *The C lead was just waiting in line until the brownies finished baking.* It's not her wedding, and she is not the decision maker. She may not have taken a business card. But she may be doing research for her own wedding a few years down the line.

Now I can send "Thank you for visiting my booth" e-mails targeted to the different kinds of leads. The managers of the event may also have a list of people who registered but didn't attend, who are then candidates for a "Missed you, but you can still order now" approach.

The goal of every speaking opportunity, bridal show, grocery store demonstration, or college book signing is to begin a conversation with the customer before the event and to carry it on afterward. Give the event persistence in time, and open as many lines of communication as possible.

Making print ads count. By now, you can probably recognize some of the mistakes I made with my Mother's Day ad of 1997. It was an isolated, one-shot event. Instead of being part of an integrated marcom campaign, it was supposed to generate sales all by itself. No direct-mail or e-mail called attention to it; its readers didn't know anything about my product beforehand. I wasn't doing a cooking demonstration at the store. I didn't offer a discount, coupons, or free delivery. Most importantly, I didn't have a testimonial.

Here are some improvements I could have made:

- *Message refinement.* Ordering over the Internet was still a new phenomenon in those days. I could have reassured the customers of the simplicity and safety of the process.
- *Testimonials.* Customer testimonials are the print equivalent of word of mouth, which is the best kind of advertising there is. I make a special effort to collect testimonials at personal appearances. Celebrity endorsements are even better. A consumer might be impressed to see that a dozen customers have bothered to write in and praise your product, but he doesn't know them personally and can't even be sure they're real. But he's probably heard of a celebrity, whose signature or image adds credibility. In my press kit, I maximize the effect of Barbara Walters's testimonial by displaying an exact copy, letterhead and all, instead of a quote (see page 153).
- *Benefit-driven content.* One of the biggest mistakes in advertisement is to focus exclusively on "image" (we're hot, we're sexy, we're high-tech, and so forth). The customer doesn't want to marry you, she wants to know how your product will benefit *her*. Your focus should always be on those benefits. My Mother's Day ad should have stressed free delivery and how much easier it would be to order online than to go down to a store, and it should have supplied the direct benefit of a coupon.

- *A well-targeted venue.* Was there any particular advantage in using a local newspaper, considering I don't have a local shop? Today, I'd advertise in a newspaper if my company was featured in the newspaper, because there would be harmony and coordination in the messages. I have advertised in show guides and onsite bridal magazines for bridal fairs I participated in. But a full-page color ad in a national bridal magazine can cost as much as $50,000, which is way out of bounds for any small business.

  I finally found a well-targeted place for a print ad while working with the Cupertino Chamber of Commerce. The chamber is a nonprofit association of 500 firms. The chamber newsletter carried a story on Luv's Brownies® that was sent to all 500 member businesses, so I took out an ad in the same issue and added a flyer with a special free-delivery offer. I was hitting them with three messages at once, and I followed up by providing a free brownie dessert at the organization's monthly mixer. At the mixer, I met reporters for the *Cupertino Courier* and the *Sunnyvale Sun* who wrote stories on my business for their papers. Clearly, I'd found the right place to advertise.

In short, I believe in paid advertising if it:

- is based on benefit-driven messages specifically targeted to your intended audience.
- includes a strong customer testimonial, such as "Best brownies I've ever tasted!"
- is carried out as part of an integrated marketing communications campaign that observes the four Ps of marketing: product, place, promotion, and price.

January 14, 1998

Ms. Aundrea Lacy
LUV'S Brownies
770 N. Winchester Blvd
#19
San Jose, CA 95128

Dear Ms. Lacy,

The brownies were absolutely fabulous! Thank you so much for sending them to my pals and I. I wish you continuing success.

Fondly,

Barbara Walters

Get Still and Listen to that Little Voice

This is a short chapter, but it's no less important than any of the other steps to success I've discussed.

When I first started Luv's, I thought I was going to lose my mind. There were so many new demands and challenges. I had a tough time keeping myself prioritized and organized and keeping some sort of social life.

I'd always been an extremist who would get either an A or an F—be either loved or hated. So at first, I threw myself into my business and let it swallow me up.

I learned—the hard way—about the virtues of balance and planning. Repeatable processes saved my life, simplified the challenges, and gave me breathing room and the perspective to work *on* my business and not *in* it.

This brings me to the second meaning of the phrase, "Your business is you." Once you make the commitment to own your own business, the ups and downs of your personal life become part of the mix. Just as you can never take the business environment for granted and must always carefully monitor the competition and the changing climate of customer needs, you can never assume that your personal life is going to follow a safe, predictable path. That just isn't what happens.

Expect to work on your life the way you work on your business. Expect that you will always have to bring order out of chaos and prioritize your time to meet your most important demands. Get your thoughts, feelings, and actions into alignment, and take action.

Just as I was building Luv's, I learned that James, the closest person to me, was infected with AIDS, and I had to handle both situations at once. Although that seems like an extreme example, the truth is that we all face life-changing crises all the time: falling in love, having babies, getting ill, and so on.

No one can avoid these crises. But you must try to manage your life as well as you manage your business. Research each new problem, as I researched James's treatment, and form a realistic action plan. For recurring problems, like paying bills, create repeatable processes to keep them simple and automatic.

As I was writing my first book, *Luv Story*, I suddenly encountered one of those life-changing events. I uncovered a family secret—the fact that I was adopted. My life was turned upside-down, and my very identity seemed to be in question. You might guess how I tackled the problem. I researched, made a plan, and took action. Within just a few weeks, I'd cut through all the red tape and discovered the facts about my adoption. Suddenly, I had a new picture of myself: I was still African-American, but I also had Hispanic ancestry—which answered questions many people had asked about my appearance all my life.

After I got over the initial surprise, I decided not to have an extremist reaction. When you manage your life the way you manage your business, you don't let other people or external forces brand and define you. My parents were the people who raised me, regardless of who gave birth to me. I have been very blessed to have parents who have loved me no matter what type of crisis has come up. The word "parents" means "teachers." My real parents are the people who raised me, taught me, and loved me, and I am their daughter. Over the next few months, that lesson continued to sink in and made me take a good look at myself and where I was going.

Meeting Mateo

I was 37 years old and had never married or had children. Most of my life I'd never wanted to; my dad told me that was because of the kind of guys I had dated—not marriage material. Before I started Luv's, I'd managed a full-time career doing marketing for high-tech firms, but I'd always had enough time to do whatever I wanted on the side: I'd modeled for print ads, I'd been a television journalist on an early-morning show, and I'd been an extra in movies. I had traveled throughout the United States, Singapore, Malaysia, Indonesia, England, Paris, the Bahamas, Puerto Rico, Hong Kong, Mexico, and other countries. I'd led a pretty full life.

One morning, I woke up and realized that I didn't want my life to be all about me. I began to research the process of adopting a child—how to go about it, what I would need to do every step of the way. I contacted the same agency that had processed me, the City and County of San Francisco adoptions unit. I registered for a two-hour informational meeting on black American adoption. A social worker came to my home to do an assessment of my temperament, family background, reasons for wanting to adopt, and so forth. I was asked to get a background check and physical. I was fingerprinted for a criminal investigation and reference check. I took an all-day class on the adoption process for five Saturdays in a row.

During the process, I learned a lot. I learned that California leads all states in out-of-home foster placements, with nearly 100,000 children involved. Between 1983 and 2000, the number of children in foster care increased by more than 300 percent. Two-thirds of the foster children awaiting permanent adoption in Alameda and San Francisco counties are black.

Older children are less likely to be adopted. Youths between 13 and 18 years old make up roughly one-third of the population in foster care, despite the fact they represent only about 12 percent of the U.S. population. The most sobering statistic: 62 percent of children who fall under the jurisdiction of the California Youth Authority are children who have been in foster care. (All statistics are courtesy of the Black Adoption Placement and Research Center in Oakland, CA.)

The more I heard, the more I realized what an important

responsibility it was to provide a permanent home for a child, and I realized how desperately I wanted to do it.

After the course was complete, a social worker came to my home to ask more questions about my background and family history. I completed the entire process in December 2005, and my finished application was submitted. The next step was to match me with a baby or child.

In March 2006, I was in Puerto Rico on vacation with my friend, Stormy. My phone beeped with a voicemail: it was the social worker, saying I had been matched with a newborn baby boy. I called her back within minutes. She gave me some information about my new bundle of joy and faxed me my baby's background and medical history.

Days later, I met with my social worker and my baby's social worker. I told them I wanted to move forward with the process as quickly as possible. I had never been so excited in my entire life—I felt almost as if I'd actually given birth.

I don't believe in luck, but God works in mysterious ways. Within days, we had the disclosure meeting—my social worker, my baby's social worker, my baby, his foster mother at that time, and me. As we were all getting to know one another, the foster mother (whom I will call Martha) asked where I was from; I told her that I was from San Francisco but raised in San Bruno.

Martha said, "There aren't too many black people in San Bruno."

I said, "I know. My dad was a hairdresser before he retired. He owned his shop for about 35 years."

Martha said, "Is your dad 'Lacy'?"

"Yes."

"Your dad is my hairdresser—he has been for years!" She realized she had known about me since I was a child. "I know your mom and both your brothers."

I sat back in complete amazement. It was at this moment I realized that God had bigger plans for me than I had for myself. Martha made me laugh by saying, "Your name threw me off. Your mom doesn't call you Aundrea. She calls you—" and she told me my family nickname.

Then I knew it was true—I couldn't stop laughing. I told her to please keep calling me Aundrea.

Within a few days of that meeting, I was able to:

- start visiting my son, with Martha, for a few hours at a time,
- take him out for two to three hours on a few different days,
- have an all-day visit, from 8 a.m. to 5 p.m.,
- and finally take him home with me overnight.

He was still just a newborn. I watched him constantly while he was sleeping. I couldn't believe my eyes. He was so beautiful. I was so proud to be his mom.

I decorated the house with balloons, put banners in the yard, and purchased a cake. I even dressed up our dog, Hot CoCo, a six-pound Maltese mix. (CoCo pretended that my new son was her baby, too.) The whole neighborhood gave me a big welcome, including visits and gifts, as soon as I brought my baby son home. Neighbors I didn't even know brought me clothes and toys. My phone rang off the hook. My dad bought formula, clothing, and diapers before I even brought the baby home—he just couldn't wait. It was as if I'd given him a million dollars.

I named my baby Mateo Sebastian. Mateo is Spanish for Matthew and means "God's gift." I believe he is truly God's gift to me—nothing as random as pure luck. There were too many coincidences.

As I got to know Mateo's social worker, whom I will call Karen, she became more and more amazed at the linkages between Mateo and me.

Karen asked, "What church did your family attend?"

"Providence Baptist Church in San Francisco."

"So did I!" she said. It turned out that Karen and I were the same age and had grown up in the same church. It's a small world, and God keeps His eye on every corner of it.

That's my story. Now that I am a single mom, I understand more than ever the value of balancing one's life and one's work. Fortunately, I have at my disposal all the tools I have taught you.

1. Research told me how to childproof my home (and my dog!).
2. Time management and personal organization methods allow me to meet the needs of Mateo's schedule as well as my own.
3. Budgeting and advance planning will be essential for his future.

The same old skills apply to the new challenges. I'm so happy to have begun this new chapter in my life.

I have four basic principles. Have fun. Use your time wisely. Work smart. And above all, believe that God, by whatever name you know Him, is always in control, even when you can't understand what He is doing.

Some hardships in life are just mysteries waiting to be solved and blessings in disguise.

Each day take some time for yourself. Get still, and listen to your heart; just as Mama Kake has often told me, it will not lead you astray. God speaks to you even when you don't want to listen. Today, I take time for myself every morning to visit my spiritual place, and I do not let anything interrupt me; whenever I've skipped this ritual, I've had an awful day. Since the day God whispered to me, "Look at your doll, Luv, and call your company Luv's Brownies—brownies shaped like hearts," I have never left my house without saying my prayers on my knees. In fact, some days I have hurried out the door a little too quickly and have had to turn the car around, pull back into the garage, and say my prayers on my knees.

My final word of advice: When that little voice speaks, don't just listen. Take action! Think of all the times your heart has spoken before, all the dreams and plans it has suggested to you, and the things you know you could have done, and should have done, with your life. It's not too late. Don't wait for the perfect day—the day you can see your whole path ahead, safe and secure. That day never comes. Get your thoughts, feelings, and actions in alignment and take charge. Start the day you get the call, pick the road you want to travel, and let God pick the place where He will join you. You will always face obstacles, but with His help, you can meet any challenge. Don't let anything keep you from making your dreams a reality.

With all of our hearts,

Aundrea and Mateo Lacy

Luv Bites® (bite-sized heart-shaped brownies) are perfect for wedding favors and parties. Luv Bites are packaged in gift tins and gift baskets. Gift tins are great gifts for Dad anytime of the year.

The 4″ heart-shaped standard brownie is a great gift, wedding favor, or a delicious part of one of our gift baskets.

About the Author

Aundrea Lacy is the founder and owner of Luv's Brownies®, an award-winning online bakery specializing in brownies shaped like hearts, which she launched in 1996 (and which she named after a favorite childhood doll called "Luv"). Her story has been featured on the Montel Williams TV show and in numerous print publications, including *Every Day with Rachael Ray,* which listed Luv's Brownies as one of her "Faves." For twenty years, Aundrea has been a marketing communications consultant in the high-tech sector, and she also gives career presentations for girls and women from around the country. She has an MBA from Golden Gate University and she mentors troubled youth as a Big Sister of Santa Clara County. Born and raised in San Francisco, she now lives in the Bay Area. Her website is www.luvsbrownies.com.